According to
the Word

This is a great book about a real hero of Christianity. We owe so much to people like John Wycliffe. He was one of the first people to translate the Bible into English, inspiring Wycliffe Bible Translators to do for others what he did for English speakers. His teaching paved the way for the Reformation, and his life inspires us to stand firm in Christ. A terrific read!'

James Poole, Executive Director
Wycliffe Bible Translators

According to the Word

John Wycliffe

David Luckman

CF4·K

10 9 8 7 6 5 4 3 2 1

Copyright © 2024 David Luckman
Paperback ISBN: 978-1-5271-1080-9
Ebook ISBN: 978-1-5271-1126-4

Published by Christian Focus Publications,
Geanies House, Fearn, Tain, Ross-shire,
IV20 1TW, Scotland, U.K.
www.christianfocus.com;
email: info@christianfocus.com

Cover design by Daniel van Straaten
Cover illustration by Graham Kennedy
Printed and bound by Nørhaven, Denmark

Contents

The Great Plague

When the *Black Death* landed on the southern shores of England in the summer of 1348[1], no one was prepared for the devastation that followed. News of millions of deaths in Europe came with the ships that sailed across the English Channel. The plague, however, sneakily came on those ships too. It was carried by black rats and the fleas which lived on their backs and feasted on their blood.

The infected rats hid in the bowels of the European ships which were bound for England. The disease ridden fleas also attached themselves to the voyagers on board and infected them with the deadly plague when they bit into their skin. A sufferer usually only lived between two and six days before death came knocking on their door. It was a very painful way to die.

When the ships disembarked, the disease was brought to shore and spread like wildfire through the population. As the plague swept northwards through England, it left thousands of people dead

---

1. See *Fact File* called 'The Black Death' at the back of the book.

in its wake. It reached the small market town of Oxford in November 1348, when John Wycliffe was a twenty-four year old student at Merton College. He had started his studies at Queen's College as a sixteen year old. Then he transferred to Merton College soon afterwards.

Colleges in the fourteenth century were only small communities, so everyone knew each other. All the colleges together made up the University of Oxford[2]. John was working hard to get a Bachelor of Arts degree, although he was still a good number of years away from achieving it. Most students or undergraduates who entered an Oxford college were only fifteen or sixteen years of age. Usually a student was over thirty years old before being awarded his degree. Nonetheless, John had an aptitude for learning new things and it didn't matter to him how long it took before he got his Bachelor of Arts. He was clever and good at studying. He would keep at it. Yes, it was safe to say that John was enjoying his education in Oxford.

However when the plague arrived in England, it impacted everyone's life in the country. The town of Oxford was no exception. Many people died there. Everyone grieved the loss of family members, neighbours and friends. For John, the continual sight of

---

2. In medieval England, the **University of Oxford** was made up of the small college communities of Balliol College, University College, Queen's College, Merton College, Exeter College, Oriel College and Canterbury College.

dead bodies being carted away to *plague pits*[3] at various locations around Oxford deeply affected him.

Lots of people believed that the plague was from God. It was his judgement on the world for being full of wickedness and sin. This rang true in John's heart too. He desperately wanted to escape the judgement to come on the Last Day. John turned to the pages of the Bible to find comfort and hope. He spent long periods of time on his knees repenting of his sins and asking God to show him the way that he should follow. He drank deeply from Scripture and found the light that he needed in the person of Jesus Christ. John repented of his sins and placed his trust in Christ. He vowed to serve the Lord all the days of his life.

During that awful time, John realised there were many people who did not know the Lord Jesus personally. They did not have the light of Scripture to guide and comfort them in their Christian lives, as he did. There were a number of plausible reasons for this. It was partly due to the fact that most ordinary people could not read at all. Therefore they could not read the 'Vulgate[4]', which was the only Bible available. It was called the 'Vulgate' because it was the most commonly used Bible at the time. The Vulgate was written in Latin. Ordinary people could not read Latin either. Latin was

---

3. A *plague pit* was a huge grave in which many people who died from plague were buried.
4. *The Vulgate*, from the Latin *editio vulgate* meaning 'common version'. It was written by a priest called Jerome in 382 A.D. at the request of Pope Damasus I.

the language of scholars and noblemen who had been given a good education. It was also very expensive to buy a copy of the Vulgate. And there were no copies of the Bible written in English which was the common language of the ordinary men and women of the land.

Sadly, there was also a sinister reason that existed for people's ignorance of the Bible. Over a hundred years previously, the church authorities had commanded that the laity[5] were not allowed to read it. They also outlawed any translation work from Latin into the English language. The Church of Rome thought there was a mystical power contained in the Latin words. They believed that any translation would take away the power of the clergy over their flock. Sadly, the clergy liked power and authority, more than serving others in humility and righteousness.

The ban against an English translation of the Bible was still in force when the plague arrived in Oxford. John Wycliffe hated this. As far as he was concerned, the ban kept people reliant on the clergy to tell them the truth about God. John believed it gave the clergy[6] too much power and control over people. It was too easy for the church to feed the population's fear of hell with sinful superstitions and then profit from them. 'Pardon for sins' could be bought at the right price, as long as the buyer had enough money.

---

5. *Laity* is the name given to people who are not members of the clergy.
6. *Clergy* is the plural word that refers to the ordained ministers of the Church.

Selling indulgences was very profitable for the clergy, monks and friars who promoted them as a way to peace with God. Indulgences were pieces of parchment that were sold to people for money. They offered pardons from purgatory – that's the place where souls were thought to suffer after death, so that they could work off some of the punishment for their sins that they committed during their lives. The clergy encouraged sinners to give money, rather than doing penance[7] for their sins. Selling indulgences was a good way to earn money. Another excellent money-spinner was taking payments so that a special Mass[8] could be said for someone's dead relative or friend. Apparently this would help the deceased to find peace in heaven.

All of these deceptions made Wycliffe angry. Did the Church of Rome really want to keep people in darkness, helpless and ignorant of the truth of God's Word? Was the church afraid of an educated and literate population who could read and understand the Scriptures for themselves? There was no doubt in John's mind that ordinary people were in bondage to the Church of Rome. John knew it wasn't right, but the Pope[9] was very powerful in England, at least for the time being.

---

7. **Penance** was a form of punishment on the body. For example, striking one's own back with a whip as a visible expression of repentance for wrongdoing.

8. **Mass** is the term given by Roman Catholics to the celebration of the death and resurrection of Jesus Christ. It is also called The Lord's Supper, Holy Communion, or The Eucharist..

9. The **Pope** is the head of the Roman Catholic Church.

John had gone to Oxford to enter the church as a 'secular clergyman', which was the description given to a priest that engaged in the normal day to day work of a parish church. The secular clergy could also be employed to do some other important work for the church in society, for example, lecture in a college. This was the path that John hoped to take.

There were also 'regular clergy' who were made up of monks and friars[10]. The difference between the two types of clergy was that the 'regular clergy' did not sit under the authority of a local bishop[11], as the secular clergy did. The 'regular clergy' were only accountable to the Pope.

A number of different communities of monks and friars existed. The Dominican friars and the Franciscan friars were the most powerful in England, especially at Oxford. These religious orders were named after their founders. At the beginning of the thirteenth century, Dominic de Guzman founded the Dominican friars. Francesco d'Assisi founded the Franciscan friars. The Dominican friars wore a black habit[12], to distinguish them from the grey habit worn by the Franciscan friars. These two men and their followers were wandering

10. **Monks** and **friars** were men who were part of a religious order or community. Monks lived in one location in a monastery, whereas friars moved around the country and stayed with other friars of their order in different places.

11. A **Bishop** is a high ranking minister who has the responsibility of overseeing churches in an area called a diocese.

12. A **habit** is a long tunic with an outer garment worn over it (called a *scapular*) and a loose hood (called a *cowl*).

penniless preachers, moving through the villages, towns, and cities of England. They modelled themselves on the disciples of Jesus who were sent out two by two to preach the gospel[13], so the friars usually travelled in pairs. They also renounced worldly riches, in keeping with the humility of the Lord. So, in order to survive, the friars begged people for provisions as they travelled and worked throughout the country.

The friars were very skilled speakers, but instead of preaching the word of God, they enchanted audiences with their imaginative stories. They did not teach the Bible, nor call men and women to repent and believe in Jesus Christ. Even the Chancellor of Oxford University, a clergyman called Richard Fitzralph, spoke strongly against the friars. Fitzralph complained bitterly to Clement VI, the Pope, that the friars were going into parishes to preach and hear the confessions of people who had committed a sin and wanted to confess it to God via a priest. The pesky friars were disrupting the proper work of the local priest. It was the priest's duty to preach and hear the confessions of his people. This work had nothing to do with the friars. In Fitzralph's opinion, the friars were a 'pestiferous cancer'– a blight on society.

When he was younger, John was respectful of the friars because he was aware of the sincerity of the men who had started these communities and who sincerely wanted to spread Christ's gospel in England. Over the years, however, the friars lost the clarity of their mission

13. Matthew 10:9-15; Mark 6:7-13; Luke 9:1-6

and message. Now they were selling 'pardons for sins' – they were notorious for it. John no longer respected them. The friars may have been good communicators, but they did not teach the Bible clearly. John viewed them as peddlers of falsehood, whose teaching only led people down the path to eternal damnation.

'The friars are a dangerous hindrance to the advance of God's kingdom on earth,' said John to a student friend, as they walked west down High Street in the direction of the castle. John was watching a couple of friars on the other side of the street perform to the crowd that had gathered around them.

'Just look at them there, pontificating their superstitions and peddling those wicked indulgences. They are keeping those poor people in the dark, when they should be showing them the light of Christ who takes away the sins of the world.' He was beginning to raise his voice at this point.

'Quietly, John,' rebuked his friend gently. 'You must be careful how you speak. The friars are everywhere in Oxford. And they have the full support of the Pope.'

'Yes, I know,' sighed John. 'It seems like I cannot walk ten yards without bumping into them!'

The two men walked ten yards further down High Street. Then John exclaimed, 'Look! There's another pair!'

'It is clear that you have no love for the friars,' said John's friend.

'I fear you are right. I have no love for the friars,' agreed John. 'What is more, one day I will let them know exactly what I think of them.'

'I have no doubt that you will, John.'

John's distrust of the friars extended to the Pope, who was in authority over them. Unlike many clergy of his day, John compared everything he saw around him with the Scriptures. And as he grew spiritually in his knowledge and love of Christ, he realised over time that the whole system of the papacy[14] was at loggerheads with the Word of God. Even the titles given to describe the Pope were contrary to the Scriptures. In Latin, the word 'Pope' means 'father', but Jesus told his disciples to call no man on earth their spiritual 'father'[15].

The Pope was also referred to as the 'Pontiff' meaning 'bridge builder', implying that he was the one who builds the bridge between humanity and God. The Bible says that only Jesus Christ bridges the gap between humanity and God[16].

Another title given to the Pope was 'Vicar of Christ'. The word 'vicar' means 'substitute' or 'representative' suggesting that the Pope was Christ's representative on earth. However, the Bible is clear that the Holy Spirit is Christ's vicar on earth[17].

---

14. **Papacy** – the office held by the Pope as the head of the Roman Catholic Church.
15. Matthew 23:9.
16. 1 Timothy 2:5-6.
17. John 14:16-17 and John 16:7.

John was greatly vexed by the Pope's blasphemy. 'If only the people could see for themselves what the Scriptures say about God. They could discern the lies told them by the papacy,' he thought. 'Lord Jesus, give me boldness to proclaim your truth, and to use the gifts you have given me for your glory,' he prayed.

The Poor Friars

John's desire was to shine the light of Christ into the darkness of his generation. To do that, first of all he had to master 'scholasticism'. This was a medieval form of education that involved learning some philosophy and theology. Debate and reasoning were the methods of teaching used to sharpen the student's mind and increase learning. And once the Bachelor of Arts degree was achieved, a student was qualified to teach others.

John got his Bachelor of Arts degree in 1358. He became a 'Fellow' of Merton College which meant he could lecture undergraduates who were studying for their own B.A. degrees. All Fellows of colleges did some lecturing. John loved teaching his students. It gave him great joy and satisfaction to know that he was helping to prepare young men for a lifetime of service to the Lord. His reputation as a fine scholar spread throughout England and he was greatly respected by people of all walks of life. He was known and admired for his love of the Bible and his submission to it as the Word of God. It transformed him to be more like his

Lord and Master, Jesus Christ. It was John's prayer that others would also be transformed through the Word and the Spirit of God. His passion for the Word of God, however, would lead John into conflict with others in the church who did not share his point of view.

John's dislike of the friars did not go away. His displeasure grew when it became known that the Franciscans were trying to lure the new students of Oxford to join them in their religious community. They offered hospitality to new students in exchange for the student's vows of obedience to the Orders of the Friars.

Richard Fitzralph was now the Archbishop[1] of Armagh in Ireland. He was so incensed about what was happening in Oxford where he was once University Chancellor, that he took the matter to the Pope. Fitzralph accused the friars of 'sheep-stealing' by using underhanded methods to entice students away from their colleges. The friars had drastically reduced the numbers of students at Oxford colleges. It was unpardonable! Although the Pope heard Fitzralph's complaint, he did nothing about it. The friars were allowed to continue their sneaky work unhindered.

John bided his time. Soon after receiving his Bachelor of Arts degree, he was elected to the grand position of Master of Balliol College. He was a fine academic and thought to be the best person to govern the college. John accepted the honour enthusiastically.

---

1. An *Archbishop* is the highest ranking bishop of a large district or area.

While in this role, the day had finally come for him to speak up against the friars, as he promised his friend all those years ago. He wrote an essay called 'Objections to the Friars'. He made his complaints against the friars public by publishing the paper in 1360.

'The friar stuffs the people only too well with rubbish,' he wrote, acknowledging that the friars were very good at communicating bad theology. But for John, the friars did not clearly nor helpfully proclaim the gospel of Christ to the people. Instead, they made long and imaginative speeches about sin. They dangled their listeners over the fires of hell and declared that hell was their listeners' destination unless they paid money to the church to have their sins absolved.

In short, John likened the friars to the religious men of Christ's day whose hearts were proud, falsely pious, and full of hypocrisy. The friars had the outward forms of religion, but their hearts and practices were deceitful and desperately wicked. They were no good at all and they did great harm to the population.

It was his pastoral concern for the people of England that moved John to attack the friars in this way. He did not want anyone hurt or led astray by the lies and superstitions of the friars. He often found himself challenging or correcting their teaching in his lectures to his students. John simply wanted all ministers of God to live under the rule of the Word of God. In fact, he wanted all people, everywhere to do the same, and know the peace and blessings of God in their lives.

John's criticism of the church made him a useful friend to the State. Since the days of King John, England wanted to be free to rule over its own affairs without interference from the Pope in Rome. This struggle for power gave John the opportunity to teach the next generation of clergy at Oxford to place their trust, not in the declarations of the Pope, but in the Word of God.

The lecture hall was unusually full the week after the publication of his book about the friars. John looked around at all the new faces in the hall. 'We seem to have increased our class size today,' he said.

Straight away a voice came from the middle of the hall. 'Master Wycliffe!' exclaimed a student. 'Why do you think the Pope has so much authority in England?'

'This is not a history class, my young friend. Today we are thinking about Augustine's view of the Trinity[2].' The group moaned softly.

'Please, Master Wycliffe,' begged a young student.

'It might help us understand your recent book a bit better,' said another.

John exhaled quietly. He hadn't planned on a history lesson. But a few minutes to explain the context of the English struggle against the papacy wouldn't hurt.

'Let us rewind the clock about a hundred and fifty years,' he began. Silence descended on the packed hall. 'The year was 1199. John, the Duke of Normandy was crowned king of England, seven weeks after the death

---

2. *Trinity* is the non-biblical word used when talking about God as 'one God in three persons' – Father, Son, and Holy Spirit.

of his brother King Richard. King John was thirty two years old. Five years into his reign the Archbishop of Canterbury died. Does anyone know who he was?'

'Master Wycliffe, it was Hubert Walter who was the Archbishop then. He died in 1205,' came a reply from an older, more mature student.

'Yes, that's correct,' affirmed John. 'An argument arose between the king and his monks about the appointment of the new Archbishop of Canterbury. The monks at Canterbury elected their leader to succeed Archbishop Walter. What happened next?'

'The king ordered them to reverse the election because he wanted to choose his own candidate,' answered a tall student on John's left.

'That's right,' said John. 'As both sides wanted their own candidate, and neither would compromise, they appealed to the Bishop of Rome[3] who was Pope Innocent III, expecting him to settle the argument. How did he do that?'

Silence. Better to say nothing and appear stupid than talk and remove all doubt.

'No one?' asked John expectantly. 'The Pope decided to ignore their elections and appoint the Archbishop himself. His choice was Cardinal Stephen Langton[4]. Does anyone know what else the Pope did?'

---

3. *The Bishop of Rome* was another name given to the Pope.
4. A *cardinal* is a senior member of the clergy in the Roman Catholic Church.

'The Pope also said that only he had the right to appoint any future Archbishop of Canterbury,' came the reply from the front row.

'Imagine that!' said John light-heartedly. 'How did King John react?'

'He was furious?' a young student sheepishly replied.

'Is that a question?' asked John. The students chuckled. 'Yes, he was very angry, and it made him paranoid too. If the Pope was willing to ignore the king's desire to appoint a new Archbishop, perhaps the Pope might want to appoint the next King of England as well.'

Every eye in the hall was looking at John, eagerly waiting for what happened next. John continued. 'As King John rejected the Pope's ruling, England was excommunicated from the family of the Church of Rome in 1207. Then what happened?'

'The Pope ordered the church in England to stop working' exclaimed an older student from the back of the hall.

'That's right!' John agreed. The younger students were shocked by that revelation from their lecturer. They couldn't believe it. John went on. 'The Pope gave the order that priests were only allowed to baptise children, as well as hear the confessions of anyone who was dying. There were no weddings or funerals.'

'What did the king do?' asked a young student who was sitting on the floor near the entrance to the hall.

'That is a good question,' said John. 'What do you think he did?' The young boy shrugged his shoulders. He had no idea. 'Does anyone know what the king did?' The hush from the students indicated that they didn't.

'Well,' began John, 'King John confiscated all church property. Then he forced the abbeys and churches to buy it back. He got a lot of money this way. But the king's actions alienated him from the church. The Pope's excommunication[5] deeply shocked the nation because their lives are revolved around the church. It was then as it is now. The people of England had never heard of a king being shunned by the church before. Can anyone tell me what Pope Innocent III did next?'

'Master Wycliffe; did the Pope encourage the French to invade England?' asked one of the older students.

'Yes, he did. By now the king's relationship with the barons[6] was at a low ebb because of how he was behaving. He could not rely on their support if the French attacked. So what did he do?'

'The king yielded to the Pope,' came the reply from a student who guessed the answer correctly.

'And?' asked John, willing the student to keep going with his answer.

'And … and …' The student was thinking hard. 'And …' No. He did not know, so John helped him.

---

5. **Excommunication** is to be excluded from or thrown out of the fellowship of the Church of Rome.

6. A **baron** was a nobleman who was given lands by the King of England. A baron served as a member of the king's council.

'And he gave up control of his kingdom to the Pope and all other popes that came after him. King John acknowledged Pope Innocent III as his superior. The king also agreed to pay a tax to the Pope of 1,000 marks[7] every year.'

'That's a lot of money, Master Wycliffe,' said a young student who was standing by the back the wall.

'Yes, it is,' replied John. 'The king also had to agree that if he or any future King of England should break the agreement, he would lose all rights to the kingdom. When the papal ambassador came to announce these terms to King John on 15th May 1213, the king took off his crown and offered it to the Pope's representative. Why did King John do that? Anybody?'

'Master Wycliffe; it was a symbol of the king putting England into the hands of the Pope.'

'Yes, very good. It was symbolic indeed. There was a ceremony of reconciliation held in Winchester Cathedral in the July of 1213. The Archbishop of Canterbury, Stephen Langton, absolved the king of his excommunication. England was now restored to the good graces of the papacy. But the barons of England were not happy. They thought the king had humiliated the nation and they did not want to be slaves to the Pope. What did the barons do?'

---

7. A **mark** was the form of currency in England at the time, worth about two-thirds of a British pound sterling today (roughly 66 pence).

'They drew up the Magna Carta[8], Master Wycliffe, and had King John sign it,' said a mature student from the middle of the student body.

'Excellent!' declared John. 'Of course, the Pope condemned the barons, and declared the charter invalid. England has struggled to obtain freedom from papal authority ever since. When King John died, the barons and the government in London discouraged future kings of England from paying the Pope's tax. If a king wanted support from the papacy, he paid the tax. If he did not need papal support, he did not pay it.'

'Is that why you wrote your book, Master Wycliffe? Do you plan to help free England from papal rule?'

John thought for a moment before answering. 'I wrote my book because unlike the friars, I am compelled to follow the example of my Lord and Master, who came into this world to seek and to save the lost. The people of England are lost without Christ. The friars are happy to keep people in fear of eternal damnation in hell, as long as they can sell their penances and line their pockets with the pennies from the poor person's purse.'

'We are poor people, Master Wycliffe!' exclaimed a young threadbare student in front of him. The other students laughed loudly.

'Yes, yes, you are poor people indeed,' John replied. 'So, hold on to your pennies! And don't give them

---

8. *Magna Carta* means *Great Charter*. The Magna Carter was the barons' statement of their rights, which they presented to King John in the summer of 1215 and made him sign it.

to those begging friars!' he said emphatically. More laughter erupted from his audience.

John raised his voice to be heard over the hubbub of the students. 'You must listen to me carefully,' he said, and waited for the mirth to die down. When he saw that they were listening to him, John spoke up. 'Your lives should be spent in service to Almighty God, who sets the sinner free by the cross of his Son Jesus Christ,' he said. 'You are to live your lives in service to the One who welcomes the forgiven sinner into his family and into a glorious kingdom in the hereafter. The kingdom of God is not ruled by sinful and greedy men who set their minds on acquiring as much power and authority as they can muster for themselves. No. It is a kingdom ruled by the loving God of the Scriptures, who loves each of you and each of those poor sinners out there in the world. And it is your duty to proclaim the gospel of Christ simply, so that people can repent of their sins, believe in him, and receive the gift of eternal life.'

The respect that the students had for Master Wycliffe was palpable, even more so after his exhortation to them to serve the Lord Jesus and to love those who are lost from him. John was a good and godly role model for the students at Oxford. Some even wanted to be like him. But not everyone did. The staff and students of the Oxford colleges planned for a lifelong ministry in the church. Some of them were cautious of associating too much with the reformer, even if they agreed with some of the things that John said about the friars.

For now, they would watch him closely.

The Oxford Scholar

John was Master of Balliol College for only a short time. In May 1361 the college offered him the parish of Fillingham in Lincolnshire. The college had the privilege of gifting some parishes in England to their Fellows, but those to whom the gift of a parish was given could no longer remain in a teaching role. It meant that John could not continue as Master of the college. One of the main reasons that the university in Oxford existed was to provide the parishes of England with well-educated clergy. The university was fulfilling its mandate and providing St Andrew's Church in Fillingham with a very scholarly and capable minister.

During the next two years in Fillingham, John fulfilled all the duties that were expected of a parish rector[1]. He knew what the role demanded, and he believed there were three vital tasks that the pastor must give his time to. The first was to feed his flock with the Word of God. The second was to remove from his flock any unhealthy thoughts and habits that are not

---

1. A *rector* is the title given to a minister in charge of a local church.

acceptable to the Word of God. The third was to defend the flock against the wolves – the false teachers - that want to attack and hurt them. 'A good pastor should take care of the souls that are in his charge,' he would often say to his young students at Oxford.

Wycliffe missed his students. He missed teaching them. He missed studying theology. It was difficult for John to be away from the small market town that he had known as home for so long. Therefore he applied for a non-residence licence, which meant that he did not have to live in the parish of Fillingham but still remain as rector. A rector could pay for a vicar[2] to take care of a parish in his absence. John paid for a vicar to look after the flock at Fillingham, and he returned to Oxford. John then rented a room at Queen's College and was given permission to study for a Master of Arts degree in theology. It was the pathway to being a Doctor of Theology, which was his goal.

John had a lot of studying and lecturing ahead of him. He set himself to the task, but in 1365 there was a distraction. That year Pope Urban V[3] demanded payment of the tribute money that had been promised by King John in the past. It hadn't been paid for years, but now he wanted it. Not only that, but the Pope also wanted the payment to be backdated to when it was last paid. That was thirty eight years ago – the sum of money he wanted was huge!

---

2. A *vicar* is a minister who is the rector's representative in a parish. The rector would pay the vicar to perform the rector's duties in the church.
3. Pronounced 'Pope Urban the Fifth.' The 'V' is the Roman numeral for the number 'five'.

The King of England, Edward III, stopped paying the annual tribute to the Pope back in 1333. Then from 1337, the country was fighting a war with France. It was part of the Hundred Years' War[4] between the two countries. King Edward was certainly not going to pay money to a French Pope who lived in the papal capital of Avignon in France[5]. Not surprisingly, King Edward did not want to risk his money being used by the Pope against his own army in the war with France.

In the same year, John was made the Warden of Canterbury Hall. It had been founded by the Archbishop of Canterbury, Simon Islip. The archbishop had appointed a monk to the post of warden, known as Henry Wodehall. He was a useless warden, so the archbishop dismissed him and asked John to take over. Three other monks that were on staff at Canterbury Hall were also replaced with three secular priests. John applied himself fully to his new post and enjoyed teaching the students there. But a storm was heading his way.

The following year Archbishop Islip died. His successor was Simon Langham, a former monk and Abbot of Westminster Abbey in London. The displaced monks of Canterbury Hall were convinced that the

---

4. *The Hundred Years' War* between England and France was not one long war, but a series of short wars. It started in 1337 and ended in 1453. For more information about the Hundred Years' War, see *Fact File* 'Hundred Years' War' at the back of the book.

5. The court of the papacy moved from Rome during the reign of Pope Clement V in 1309. See *Fact File*, 'The Avignon Papacy'.

new archbishop would listen favourably to their plight. Archbishop Langham came to the decision that his predecessor was wrong in the way that he dismissed Wodehall and his other staff of monks. The archbishop expelled John from his wardenship. He dismissed the other three scholars as well. Then he reinstated Wodehall and his three monks to their former positions at Canterbury Hall.

There was no way that John was going to let such an injustice prevail. As Archbishop Langham held the highest position in the church in England, John had to make his appeal to get reinstated as Warden of Canterbury Hall to Pope Urban V who lived in Avignon, France. The Pope was in no hurry to decide John's case. Popes were notorious for taking a long time to make decisions like this.

In the meantime, King Edward assembled a parliament in 1366 to address the issue of the papal taxation. It met in the beautiful Palace of Westminster situated on the north bank of the River Thames in the centre of London. Because he was a chaplain to the king, John was invited to be present. Edward knew that John was the ablest scholar in the land. It was decided that John should respond to the Pope on behalf of the king and parliament of England. John listened carefully to the discussion between the barons and other nobles of the land.

'The kingdom of England was won by the sword,' said a military baron. 'By that sword, England has been defended. Let the Pope then put a sword on his belt and come and try to take his tribute by force. I am ready to resist him, even if no one else is.' The assembly erupted with cheers of agreement.

Then another baron stood up and said, 'The Pope is a minister of the gospel. He does not rule a country. It is his duty to give us spiritual counsel, not physical protection from our enemies. Let us encourage him to operate within the limits of his spiritual office, and if he does we shall obey him. But if he chooses to cross over the boundary of these limits, he must take the consequences for it.' Another loud cheer went up from the parliament.

John noticed how united the parliament seemed to be against the papacy. It was quite remarkable to witness such unity in the political life of England. The third baron who spoke said, 'The Pope calls himself the "servant of the servants of God". What service has England ever received from the man who bears such a title as this? Not spiritual edification that's for sure! Rather, he takes our treasures to make himself and his court in Avignon rich, while he shows favour and gives advice to our enemies.'

Another incensed baron declared, 'To give away spiritual benefits for money is a piece of papal swindling!' And he encouraged all the lords of the land to oppose such a disgraceful transaction.

'Pope Urban tells us,' began another baron, 'that all kingdoms are Christ's and that he as his 'vicar' holds

England for Christ. However, the Pope is capable of sinning, and he may abuse his trust. So it appears to me that it would be better if we should hold our land directly and alone for Christ.'

The barons and nobles were of the same mind. Yet it was the last comment which struck at the heart of the issue for many of them. 'Let us go at once to the root of this matter,' said the final speaker. 'King John had no right to give away the kingdom of England without the consent of the nation. That consent was never given. The golden seal of the king and the seals of a few nobles whom John coerced to join him in this transaction, do not constitute the national consent. If John gifted his people to Pope Innocent III as if they were possessions, the Pope may come and take his property if he can. We, the people of England, had no voice in the matter. We hold the bargain completely invalid from the beginning.'

The deafening cries of approval rang throughout the chamber. John was in no doubt of the unanimous decision that parliament would give to Pope Urban V in relation to his tribute demands. John took careful note of the verdict of parliament, which basically said that no king could bring his kingdom into bondage like that, without the assent of his people. King John had gone against his kingly oath at his coronation to serve and protect his subjects. Therefore, if the Pope attempted anything against the king, then it was only reasonable that the king along with all his subjects, should resist the Pope with all their force and power. His own view was similar.

It was a feisty but productive gathering. The Pope managed to do something that many thought impossible – he united the parliament of England! Parliament decided that King Edward must not pay the money. Should the pontiff go ahead with his threat, then the king would have all the power and resources of the nation placed at his disposal to defend his crown and the honour of England.

Not long after the meeting of parliament, John received a message from a monk who was in favour of the Pope's actions. The monk tried to defend the Pope's demands in a letter, and he challenged John to answer his arguments, if he was able to. John liked a challenge. He started to read the monk's communication.

The monk argued that, 'As the Pope is superior to all monarchs, and the supreme lord of their kingdoms …'

John stopped reading. 'That is a very grand claim,' he thought. Then he read on to see what conclusions the monk reached after so bold a beginning to his letter.

'No matter who they are, all monarchs owe the Pope obedience and tribute. Moreover, submission to the Pope was especially due from the English monarch as a consequence of the surrender of the English kingdom to the Pope by King John. Without doubt, King Edward III had clearly surrendered his throne by not paying the annual tribute to the Pope. One more thing,' wrote the monk. 'All clergy are exempt from the power of the courts and are under no obligation to appear before the powers of the State.'

These arguments were not hard for John to answer, although he knew that he was about to attack the papacy, the greatest power in the world at the time. He sat at his desk in the room of his Queen's College residence and started to write his response on behalf of King and country. He called his response the 'Determination'. He wanted to truly reflect parliament's view concerning the papal tribute And, as a chaplain to the King, Wycliffe was in a position to speak with authority.

'Already a third and more of England is in the hands of the Pope,' John replied, referring to the amount of land and property owned by the Roman Church in England. 'There cannot be two temporal rulers in one country,' he said. 'Either Edward is king or Urban is king. We, the people of England, make our choice. We accept Edward of England and refuse Urban of Rome.' John was clever in highlighting to the monk that the disagreement was not between the monk and himself, but rather it was between the King of England and Pope Urban V. If England bowed before Rome, what country could ever free itself from the bondage of Rome? He concluded his 'Determination' by saying that the condition imposed by the Pope and accepted by King John all those years ago was a 'vain thing', and he challenged the monk to prove that it was not.

When the 'Determination' was published, John lost favour with Rome. He expected this. The king, barons, and people of England, however, loved him for standing up to the Pope on their behalf. From now on, John was the spokesman for England in matters of religion. He would champion the rights of the people of England against the papacy.

Not surprisingly, John's case for reinstatement as Warden of Canterbury Hall was left to drag on for an incredible four years. In 1370 Pope Urban concluded that Archbishop Langham was right to re-appoint Wodehall and the three monks to their former posts. John had lost his wardenship. He was very disappointed with the decision.

On the plus side, he had helped to save England from further slavery to the whims of Rome.

The Evangelical Doctor

John opened the door of his room to a welcomed face. Nicholas Hereford was a Fellow of Queen's College. Most importantly he was a good friend to John at a time when other clerical colleagues were keeping their distance.

'Please come in, Nicholas,' said John.

'I hope that I am not disturbing you, John,' Nicholas said.

'No, not at all. I was just doing some work for my doctorate,' admitted John. Nicholas walked into the room and sat on a chair that was in the corner of the room. John took his chair from behind his desk and positioned it close to his friend. 'Did you read the "Determination"?' he asked as he sat down.

'Most certainly I did.'

'How has it been received in Oxford?'

Nicholas drew breath as he thought carefully about his next words.

'There is no doubt that most of the clergy, monks and friars think you are a traitor to the Pope in Avignon, John.'

'I thought as much.'

'Although,' added Nicholas, 'I have heard that the nobility are thrilled to have a priest who has the brains and the brawn to risk the Pope's displeasure in defence of England.'

'It feels like all eyes are now on Oxford,' said John.

'And they are,' agreed Nicholas. 'Neither the king nor the Pope can do anything without the people asking, 'What will Wycliffe say?!'

John was stunned to hear this. Then both men chortled. It was not John's intention to make a name for himself. He was only seeking to obey the will and the Word of God in all things.

'John, what will you do now that you have the ear of parliament?' Nicholas asked.

'I will continue to use what little influence I have for the good of the nation and the advance of the kingdom of God in these fair lands,' John replied.

'I am sure you will,' affirmed his good friend. 'What does your patron think of it all?'

'The Duke of Lancaster? I haven't spoken to him for a while. He was quite indignant when he heard that Pope Urban V was seeking backdated annual tributes.'

'I suspect he is pleased that England has stood her ground against further papal taxations.'

John nodded. 'I suppose he is,' he said.

Nicholas then changed the subject slightly. 'You never did mention how King Edward's son became your patron[1].'

'Did I not?' John rose from his seat and walked to a chest of drawers on which a jug of water and two empty goblets sat. He poured some water into the goblets. 'There is not much to tell,' he began. 'I met John of Gaunt, the Duke of Lancaster[2] a number of years ago.' John walked back to his seat and handed a goblet of water to his friend and sat down. 'As King Edward's son, he had lands throughout England, including a little village in West Riding, up in Yorkshire where I grew up.'

'So when he became your patron, it was likely that he knew of your origins on his lands?'

'Most likely,' said John, and took a sip of water from his goblet.

Usually John did not speak much about his relationship with John of Gaunt, the king's third son. Although patronage was the usual way to get ahead in the world at the time, John had one of the most powerful men in England as a patron. In fact, John of Gaunt was practically ruling the country because King Edward III was old and sick. The king's firstborn and heir, Edward of Woodstock, had just returned home from fighting in France. He was nicknamed 'the Black Prince' because he wore black armour in battle and had

1. A *patron* is someone who protects and supports another person. A *protégé* is someone who receives protection and support from a patron.
2. For more information about *John of Gaunt*, see the *Fact File* at the back of the book.

spent a lot of time overseas waging war. He too was ill and in no fit state to take control of the king's affairs. The king's second son, Lionel of Antwerp, had died a few years earlier in 1368 after a short illness. So, John of Gaunt, the king's third son, rose to prominence and power in England.

'John of Gaunt is certainly a good friend to have on your side at the moment,' Nicholas said.

'Why? Because he is a powerful man who approved of my "Determination"?' retorted John.

'Perhaps he can afford you some protection from any more of the Pope's threats in England.'

'Even if John of Gaunt cannot, Nicholas, the Lord's will will be done. I shall go on to speak the truth by the grace that God has given me.'

Nicholas rose to his feet. 'I am glad to see you, John. I shall leave you to get back to your studies.'

'Thank you for your visit, Nicholas. It is always good to see you, my friend. I shall speak with you later.' He walked Nicholas to the door and bade him farewell. He pulled his chair back to his desk and settled down to study for the rest of the day.

***

John was awarded the degree of Doctor of Divinity in 1372. It was a unique honour and a well-deserved award to the foremost scholar in England. All his hard work and study had paid off. He was also given the title of 'Professor of Divinity' which allowed him to open up his own lecture hall in the university and teach any student who wanted to attend.

It was not uncommon for a Doctor of Theology to be given a special name, or a term of endearment, by the academic community. In the past some teachers received names such as 'Doctor Angelicus' (Angelic Doctor), or 'Doctor Profundus' (Profound Doctor) perhaps because of some good personal attribute or wise thinking that the scholar possessed. John was called 'Doctor Evangelicus' (Evangelical[3] Doctor), because he constantly talked about the good news of Jesus Christ in his lectures to his students and in his writings.

It was common for academics like John to write a lot of books. One book in particular that John wrote was very helpful for understanding who God is and how he wants his people to live a life of true freedom. The book was a clear explanation about the Ten Commandments[4] from the Bible. John believed that many who wanted to call God 'Master' and who professed to honour Jesus were very ignorant of the Ten Commandments. John wanted to teach them about the Lord who rescues his people and teaches them how to be truly free, by saying things like, 'You shall have no other gods before me[5]' and 'Honour your father and your mother[6]'.

---

3. The word *Evangelical* is from the Greek word *euangelion* which means good news or gospel.

4. The *Ten Commandments* can be found in Exodus 20:1-17.

5. Exodus 20:3.

6. Exodus 20:12.

John wrote, 'The Bible is clear when it says that it is the obligation of all people to honour and love God supremely. To this end it is necessary that everyone should hear the commandments of God publicly read, preached, and taught, and then do what God says[7].'

He thought, 'It's the only way to be truly free from telling lies and coveting things that are not yours and from being enslaved by your own desires. When people indulge their own selfish desires, it leads to broken lives, broken relationships, and broken hearts. How insufferable we become in our selfishness!'

At times John lamented at the spiritual apathy that he witnessed in people all over the country, so he wrote it down in his book too. 'But what person is there now-a-days that dreads to break God's commandments, or is duly attentive to the sweetest word or the sharpest word in all God's law? Dear God, it is a wonder of all wonders on earth, that from the beginning of our life even to our last end, we are never weary, either night or day, to work hard to get worldly goods which are pleasing to our wretched body but only last for a little while. Yet when it comes to learning God's commandments, which shall be our food and nourishment to our souls that shall last in bliss or in pain, about such things we do not truly work hard for, even one hour of the day.'

---

7. From John's book about the Ten Commandments, called '*Exposition of the Decalogue*'

As John worked through the Commandments, the abuses of the church were not far from his mind. Towards the end of his work on the Ten Commandments, John wrote this: 'Many think that if they give a penny to a pardoner[8], they shall be forgiven for breaking all the commandments of God, and therefore they take no heed to keep them. I tell you for certain that even though you hire priests and friars to pray for you, and even though you go to Mass every day, and build chapels and colleges, and go on pilgrimages all your life, and give all your worldly goods to the pardoners, all this shall not bring your soul to heaven.'

It was a common practice to 'give a penny to a pardoner'. People really did believe that they could buy their way into heaven. Holding this view simply made a mockery of the cross of Christ? Why would Jesus die on the cross in the sinner's place if there was some other way to get into heaven? Dr Wycliffe had a word to say about the friars who peddled such lies in particular.

'The friars break all the commandments of God. If they want to be ruled by the laws of man rather than the commands of Christ, then they have chosen to worship false gods. They are heretics[9] and they speak against the glorious name of God. When they do this, they break

---

8. A *pardoner* is someone who pronounces 'pardon from sin' for the price of a penny, such as a priest or a friar.

9. For John Wycliffe, a heretic was someone who taught something contrary to the Bible. However, when the Pope, prelates and clergy called someone a heretic, they meant someone who taught something contrary to the teachings and traditions of the Church of Rome.

the first commandment of God that says, "I am the Lord your God. You shall have no other gods except me" (Exodus 20:2-3). They fear men and demons more than Almighty God. In their pride, they preach to receive praise from others. They corrupt God's Word. They do not preach the simple gospel of Christ, and therefore they do not win men's souls for heaven.'[10]

Often John would charge his students not to be like the false teachers that plagued the church. Instead he exhorted them to 'Have a remembrance of the goodness of God, how he made you in his own likeness, and how Jesus Christ who is both God and man, died such a painful death upon the cross to buy your soul out of hell, even with his own heart's blood, and to bring that soul to the bliss of heaven.'

The quiet longing of John's heart was for everyone in the church, whether Pope, bishop, clergy, or laity, to think this way about Christ. How different Europe and England might be if the true gospel of Jesus was believed, and the Word of God proclaimed clearly by those who said they belonged to him.

Sadly this was not the way things were. The reality was that another battle involving the papacy was heading John's way. King and country would require the services of the 'Evangelical Doctor' once again.

---

10. Paraphrased from *De Hypocritarum Imposture* – a commentary on the text 'Beware of the Leaven of the Pharisees' (Matthew 16:6) – in *Tracts and Treatises of John De Wycliffe, D.D.*, edited by Rev. Robert Vaughan for The Wycliffe Society, 1845, page 7.

The King's Commissioner

It had rained non-stop for two days in Oxford, which was good for the vegetables in the garden, but bad for the local pedestrian. The narrow streets of Oxford were usually dirty because open sewers ran down the middle of them. The recent downpour just made the streets extra muddy and super smelly.

All the buildings that lined the streets of the town had thatched rooftops, some of which let in almost as much water as they kept out. Keeping warm and dry during a hard rainfall was a difficult task in a thatched house with no chimney. If the inhabitants didn't choke from the build-up of smoke in the house, they gagged on the ferocious odour from the street outside their front door.

A messenger's horse waded its way through the stinky sludge en route for the residence of Dr Wycliffe at Queen's College. The man wore an open-sided garment with the royal coat of arms on it, which identified him as a messenger of the Crown. In his bag he had an important letter that was sealed with the king's insignia. It was the messenger's duty to hand the letter directly to Dr Wycliffe and await a response.

John greeted a sodden yet cheery servant of the king when he opened the door of his room.

'Dr Wycliffe, I have an important letter for you from His Majesty, King Edward,' said the messenger.

'Won't you come in?' asked John. 'I have a towel here somewhere; you can dry yourself,' he said, turning his head to locate the towel's position in the room.

The messenger looked at his feet as if to say, 'my pattens[1] are filthy; you really don't want me traipsing dirt into your room, Dr Wycliffe.'

'Come, come; take a seat,' John insisted. 'Never mind the dirt on your shoes. It can be easily brushed up later when it dries.'

As the door closed, the messenger removed the letter from his bag and handed it to John. Then he walked to the chair in the corner of the room, his shoes squelching with each footstep, and sat down. The little towel was hanging over the back of the chair. The young man removed it and started to dry his face.

The letter in John's hand was a request from the king to attend a meeting in London. The king and parliament had need of Dr Wycliffe's academic skills once again. It was another battle with the papacy, this time on the issue of 'papal provisions'.

John went to his desk to compose a short reply. In it he indicated his immediate departure from Oxford, and

---

1. *Pattens* were shoes worn in medieval times.

the honour he felt to be of service to king and country once again. John handed the reply to the messenger and thanked him for his service. The man rose quickly and replaced the damp towel on to the back of the chair. He took the letter gently and carefully put it in his bag. He bade Dr Wycliffe goodbye and squelched out of the room. He had a long journey back to London in the rain.

John watched the messenger leave on horseback. He decided to look for his friend, Nicholas Hereford, and tell him about the letter from the Crown. Perhaps Nicholas had some wise words of advice for him.

Nicholas had just delivered a lecture in one of the halls and was doing his best to avoid the muckiest parts of the pathways on his way to the library at Queen's College. John found him looking intently for a book. A few students seeking shelter from the rain were huddled in the far corner of the library. Nicholas did not hear his friend approach.

'Nicholas, I am glad I found you,' said John quietly. Nicholas turned round, slightly startled by his friend's voice in his ear.

'John, you made me jump,' Nicholas said. 'How are you? I wonder how long this rain will keep falling.'

'Hopefully not too much longer now,' John replied politely. 'Have you got a moment?'

'Yes, of course,' said Nicholas cheerfully. 'Let's sit down.' He pointed to a vacant table and chairs nearby.

'I have just received a communication from the Crown requesting my presence in London,' John began.

'Oh, that sounds interesting,' said Nicholas. 'Do you know why?'

'I think I am to speak on behalf of king and country once more.'

'Against the papacy?'

'Yes. I believe so.'

'How long has it been since the last time?'

Nicholas was referring to the time when John defended the nation against Pope Urban V's demand for the annual tribute.

John thought for a moment. 'It was about eight years ago, I think,' he said.

'Yes, yes. That's when Pope Urban V was the head of the church. He died four years ago.'

'Yes. In 1370. Anyway, on this occasion, it is the issue of 'papal provisions' that will be challenged.'

'Ah, papal provisions,' repeated Nicholas, 'the ability of the Pope to appoint someone of his choosing to a benefice² in England any time he wants.'

'That is right,' affirmed John, 'and when the Pope 'provides' someone, it is usually one of his favourite clergy to the benefice.'

'Usually a wealthy benefice, too,' said Nicholas.

'And the Pope can raise a princely sum of money from the annates³ that he imposes on those benefices,' added John.

---

2. A *benefice* is a church position which gives an income to a clergy-man.

3. *Annates* were taxes imposed by the Pope that usually amounted to the first year's income of a clergyman or bishop.

'I imagine the king is not pleased that more English money finds its way into the papal treasure chest in France,' said Nicholas.

'No, he is not, especially when the money can be used by the Pope to help fund the French war against England.'

'Horrific,' said Nicholas.

'Last year, the king sent some commissioners[4] to the new Pope in Avignon, Gregory XI[5].

'Oh? Any one I know?'

'Bishop Gilbert of Bangor in Wales was the lead negotiator. A monk called Bolton, I think his name is. And two laity, I believe.'

'I have heard of Gilbert, but not Bolton.'

'They were instructed to demand the Pope stop reserving benefices for his foreign candidates in the English Church.'

'I have heard around Oxford that many of the appointments over here in recent years have been given to Italians and Frenchmen,' Nicholas said. 'John, they are ignorant of the English language, and even Latin! A lot of them don't even work in their own parishes. They appoint the cheapest vicars they can get and have the rest of their income shipped back to them in Rome, or wherever else they are living. I do not think this is right, John.'

---

4. **Commissioners:** They were a group of clergy tasked by the king to represent his opinions concerning papal provisions in England.

5. Pronounced 'Pope Gregory the Eleventh'. 'XI' are Roman numerals for the number eleven.

'The commissioners were instructed to tell the Pope to stop meddling in our appointments. As far as we were concerned, the Archbishop of Canterbury had the authority in England to approve elected candidates to a bishop's position. It used to happen this way years ago.'

'Didn't parliament try to stop the Pope's interference in England before?' asked Nicholas.

'Yes, it did. The laws of 'Provisors and Praemunire'[6] were passed by parliament some twenty years back. They were designed to stop the Pope from taking control of wealthy positions in the church in England. It was hoped that by restricting the Pope's influence, it would stop the flow of money from here to the Vatican. But these laws never really worked. Parliament urged the king to do something about it. So the commissioners were sent last year.'

'What was the outcome of their negotiations?'

'As you might expect, they got nowhere.'

'Perhaps the king and parliament want to try again, with you involved,' suggested Nicholas.

'Yes, that is what I think too.'

Nicholas placed his hand on his friend's shoulder. 'Well, John, in my humble opinion, they could not get a finer advocate for truth and honour.'

John smiled. 'You are most kind,' he replied.

'I assume you will go immediately?'

---

6. See *Fact File* at the back of the book for information about 'Provisors and Praemunire'.

'Yes. I handed my reply to the messenger, and he has left for London already.'

'Then you must get ready, John. Your involvement on behalf of the Crown and parliament will not prove popular with the papacy in Avignon, or even the clergy here in England.'

'I have experienced the deep saving grace of Christ in my life, Nicholas. The Word of God says, "Christ Jesus came into the world to save sinners."[7] I am a sinner, Nicholas, saved by his grace to me through faith in Jesus Christ. Even if all men should abandon me, Nicholas, Christ Jesus will never leave me nor forsake me. "The Lord is my helper; I will not fear; what can anyone do to me?"[8]'

'I shall pray for you as you undertake this task,' said Nicholas. He rose to his feet. 'Come now. You need to go.'

***

The two scholars were right in their assessment of the situation. John was asked to be part of a Royal Commission along with Bishop Gilbert of Bangor, and a number of other negotiators. 'The purpose of the commission was to look for a way that would stop the Pope from appointing his foreign candidates to clergy positions in England. This would also put an end to any papal taxes on new clergy being exported from England to France.'

---

7. 1 Timothy 1:15.
8. Hebrews 13:5-6.

On this occasion the Pope sent his diplomats to meet with the Royal Commission in the commercial metropolis of Bruges, in Belgium. Bruges was a bustling city with a good reputation for trade. It attracted merchants from all over Europe so that the population of Bruges grew to over thirty thousand people. John had not been outside England before. He thought the enormity of Bruges made the market town of Oxford seem very small. He would look around the city a bit more if he had the time. But for now, he was focused on the task in hand.

Wycliffe was aware that another meeting involving English ambassadors was already taking place in Bruges. As the war raged on, John of Gaunt and some other diplomats were engaged in peace negotiations with representatives from France. Now that there were dignitaries not only from the papacy, but also from England and France in Bruges, it seemed sensible to engage them in two different sets of talks while they were all together in the one place.

The Bishop of Bangor and Dr Wycliffe met with the papal ambassadors to discuss the issue of the Pope's appointments in England. Pope Gregory XI firmly upheld his right as the 'landlord and owner' of England. As far as he was concerned, the king was only his tenant - it had been this way for centuries and nothing had changed. The Pope was willing for some slight compromise regarding appointments to English benefices. However, he wasn't willing to relinquish all control of appointments to the English monarchy. Instead, he insisted on having equal power with the English king over the appointments to English benefices.

The discussions between the papal diplomats and the English commissioners lasted two years. John felt the outcomes of the talks were unsatisfactory and so he concluded that he had wasted two years of his life. On the positive side, he was now more fully aware of his foe. He had seen the corruption of the men that surrounded the Pope with his own eyes. He had heard their lies with his own ears. Now he had a better idea of what he was fighting.

When the commissioners returned to England, Bishop Gilbert was given a promotion. He became the Bishop of Hereford, by means of those 'papal provisions' that he was supposedly arguing against. It seemed that his power and wealth in the English church were increasing. John couldn't believe it when he heard about Gilbert's promotion from the Pope. Perhaps this was why the talks didn't get very far. The other commissioners felt that Gilbert's promotion reeked of betrayal.

Wycliffe was not destined to climb the heights of ecclesiastical advancement. He was promised the bishopric of Worcester but was then passed over for another clergyman – one who had not taken such a contrary stance to the Pope. Instead John resigned his position as the rector of Ludgershall church and became the rector of Lutterworth in Leicestershire. This appointment did not come from the Pope, but from the king, in recognition of John's faithful service to the nation. He remained the rector of that fine parish for the rest of his life.

This was God's plan for John. Had he become the Bishop of Worcester, perhaps he would not have had the time to give to the amazing work that lay before him. God always knows what is best for his children, even when his children do not see it at the time.

Wycliffe's desire to put the Bible into the hands of ordinary people still raged in his heart. One day, by God's grace, he would make it happen.

The Papal Adversary

Bishop Gilbert was pleased with the result in Bruges, although the compromise that was negotiated in those talks did not go down well with parliament in England. In 1376 the members of parliament came together to talk about papal demands once more. The members were united in their condemnation of the papacy.

'God has given his sheep to the Pope, to be pastured, and not to be shorn or shaven!' they declared. It was their way of saying that the Pope wasn't looking after the people of God properly; that he took advantage of them by taking their money and feeding them lies about the way to heaven.

Parliament also declared that the only way to protect England from complete destruction at the hands of Rome, was to strenuously oppose any further church appointments made by the Pope for the country. 'We must ensure that no papal tax collector should stay in England upon pain of life and limb,' the members stated. 'In the same way, no Englishman should become a papal tax collector either,' they added.

This meeting of parliament became known as the 'Good Parliament' by the people of England, mainly because its members were so united in their opposition to the Pope's demands. The strength of resistance was uncanny especially during a time when the vast population of Europe only knew the spiritual leadership of the Pope and no other.

Perhaps it was John's advice to parliament that helped influence their strength of feeling and the stance England was now taking against the papacy. In a document called 'Bundle of Weeds, John advised the government that the realm of England should withhold taxes from the Pope in order to defend herself. John argued in this document that all things have the right to preserve themselves. The government has a duty of care to those whom it governs, by defending the prosperity of the realm of England. So it was completely unreasonable to expect England to give money to the French Pope because he would use it to fund the French army in its efforts to kill English soldiers and defeat England in war. It was Wycliffe's view that the Pope could only tax the nation if it was for good and godly purposes, like feeding and caring for the poor. Therefore the Pope had no right to enforce a taxation on the nation if it was not. And should the Pope feel upset by the government's decision not to fulfil his demands, he could excommunicate England from the Holy Roman Empire. But this would not be fair and therefore God would not pay any attention to it.

John was very patriotic. His convictions were clearly the same as those of parliament. Pope Gregory XI was furious when he learned of the English response to the Bruges negotiations. He tried to appoint an Italian priest to a church post in England as a mark of defiance. However parliament stood its ground and would not allow the appointment to be made. The nobility of England was also supportive of the monarchy in the stand against the power of the papacy. It appeared that Wycliffe had galvanised the nation. He was a national champion, again.

Having returned from Bruges more convinced than ever that the Pope and his cohorts were dishonest men, he started to criticise the papacy even more in his lectures. He referred to Pope Gregory XI as the 'Anti-Christ[1], the proud, worldly priest of Rome.' He did not mince his words. All the while, Wycliffe's influence in England was growing.

The hierarchy of the Roman Church was mad with John. He had defended England against Rome. No one had ever done that before. The only course of action was to strike back at him. They looked carefully at John's writings to see if they could condemn him for any false teaching. John taught the Scriptures clearly. John pointed out clearly that the Roman Church was not practicing what the Bible taught.

John was really getting under the skin of the Pope. Sitting in a richly ornate chair in his private chambers

---

1. 1 John 2:18-22; 1 John 4:3 and 2 John 7.

Pope Gregory XI met with some frustrated cardinals who were pacing up and down the room as they read out snippets of Wycliffe's writings.

'Your Holiness, this is from his book called *On Civil Dominion*,' grumbled a portly cardinal. 'He says that Christ did not give your grace any authority or supremacy over kings. England does not belong to your Holiness. Your Holiness is only a man, and therefore subject to sin.'

'How dare he say such things!' spat an angry cardinal who was standing next to Pope Gregory. 'Has he forgotten that His Holiness is the Vicar of Christ on earth?' he blustered.

'Let me hear more,' said Gregory calmly to the angry man. Indicating to the portly cardinal that he should continue with what he was reading. Which he did, stuttering.

'He ... he ... says ... he says that your Holiness has no more power to excommunicate or forgive men of their sins than any other ordinary priest in the church.'

'Holy Father, how much more of this must we endure?' asked the angry cardinal. 'You are no ordinary priest,' he added.

'No more interruptions,' commanded Gregory. 'Go on!' He glared sternly at the portly cardinal.

'Well, a bit further on he says that the monarchies of Europe cannot keep giving money to the Church of Rome *ad infinitum*. And not only that, if the money was ever abused by your Holiness, the monarchy had the right to get the money back!'

'Get the money back?!' Pope Gregory was apoplectic. John's words were intolerable to him.

'This Wycliffe is a master of errors,' Gregory asserted 'He has run into a kind of detestable wickedness, not only openly publishing but vomiting out of the filthy dungeon of his breast, this false testimony, and wrong conclusions about me. Write that down!' demanded the Pope as he glared at the angry cardinal who scrambled for some parchment and a quill. 'Make sure you get every word!' bellowed Gregory. 'The teachings of Dr Wycliffe are the most wicked and damnable heresies,' he continued. 'Indeed, he might defile the faithful Catholic people of England and bring them headlong into hell if his teachings are not stopped.'

'Yes, Your Holiness, you are absolutely right!' affirmed the angry cardinal, looking up from his frantic scribblings.

'Be quiet!' ordered Gregory. 'I do not need your flattering words.' Immediately the angry cardinal turned into a sheepish cardinal in response to the Pope's rebuke.

Back in England, the bishops were also enraged by Wycliffe's attack on the church. Not only that, but they were also worried about the growing power of the Duke of Lancaster, John of Gaunt. The duke's views about the Pope's interference in the English church were the same as Wycliffe's.

In the past, the duke wanted to limit the power of the English bishops who held top positions in the government of England. He managed to have them removed from their posts in government and replaced with law officers of the Crown. The duke's power grew stronger at the expense of the bishops. They hated him for it. Clearly something had to be done about Gaunt and Wycliffe.

The Archbishop of Canterbury, Simon Sudbury summoned Wycliffe to appear before him and the Bishop of London, William Courtenay, at St Paul's Cathedral in London on 19th February, 1377.

The news of Wycliffe's trial travelled quickly. A great crowd gathered at the doors of St Paul's. Unknown to the archbishop, Wycliffe would not face his accusers alone. John of Gaunt and Lord Henry Percy, the King's Marshal, accompanied him. Gaunt managed to bring along four Masters of Divinity to side with Wycliffe. Some of Gaunt's armed men were there as well.

Wycliffe and his companions were jostled as they slowly made their way into the cathedral and up the aisle. The trial was to take place in the Lady Chapel located on the south side of the chancel[2] of St Paul's.

'Do not let the sight of these bishops make you shrink a hair's breadth in your profession of faith, for they are unlearned men,' Gaunt said to Wycliffe. 'As for this crowd of people, fear nothing, we are here to defend you.'

Wycliffe did not reply. He was focused on facing his accusers. Bishop William Courtenay then emerged

---

2. The *chancel* is the area of a church building near the table used for the Lord's Supper, where the clergy and the choir can be seated.

from the Lady Chapel. As the men approached Courtenay, the first clash between the bishop and the two noblemen erupted. Courtenay addressed the King's Marshall first.

'Lord Percy, if I had known what authority you had in the church, I would have stopped you from coming here today!' shouted Courtenay angrily.

'He shall keep such authority here, even if you say "no",' replied Gaunt before Lord Percy could get a word out.

Wycliffe was able to see the group who had gathered for his trial. There were dukes and barons sitting with the archbishops and other bishops. Wycliffe stood before them. His appearance was sombre. He wore his long cloak of black cloth that all the doctors, ministers and students of Oxford wore. His demeanour was earnest, and his lips were firmly closed. Lord Percy and John of Gaunt sat opposite Wycliffe's accusers.

'Sit down, Wycliffe,' said Lord Percy, motioning to a vacant chair next to him. 'You have many things to answer to and have need to rest yourself on a soft seat.'

'He must and shall stand!' exploded Courtenay. 'It is unreasonable that someone who is summoned to appear before a bishop should sit down during his trial!'

'Lord Percy's proposal is very reasonable,' interrupted Gaunt. Looking sternly at Courtenay, Gaunt said, 'as for you, my lord bishop, who are grown so proud and arrogant, I will bring down the pride, not of you alone, but of all the prelacy[3] in England.'

'Do your worst, sir,' dared Courtenay.

'Look at you, standing behind the good reputation of your parents. But know this; your parents reputation shall not be able to protect you. They have enough to do to help themselves,' replied Gaunt angrily.

'My confidence,' replied Courtenay, 'is not in my parents nor in any other man, but only in God, in whom I trust, and by whose assistance I will be bold to speak the truth!'

Gaunt baulked at the hypocrisy of Courtenay's words. As far as Gaunt was concerned, the Bishop of London was not interested in the truth, because if he was, there would not be a trial of the good and patriotic Wycliffe. Gaunt was getting nowhere with Courtenay. In frustration, he turned to one of his men and exclaimed, 'Rather than take these words from the bishop's mouth, I will pluck him out of the church by the hair on his head!'

The heated words and raised voices resonated throughout the vast cathedral. The crowd heard Gaunt's threat against Courtenay and burst into the Lady Chapel. It was mayhem as Gaunt's men tried to hold back the citizens of London, but they were unable to. The meeting was overwhelmed by the people and therefore the trial was abandoned. The bishops and

---

3. *Prelacy* refers to those who are in high church office, e.g. a bishop or a cardinal.

nobles retreated to safety within the back rooms of the cathedral. Lord Percy and John of Gaunt grabbed hold of Wycliffe and escaped through the crowd and out into the streets of London.

There was no point hanging around London for another trial date. Wycliffe returned to Oxford and got on with his work there. The trial at St Paul's was an unsatisfactory outcome for him. He had always maintained that he had no desire to be a dissident and unorthodox voice in England.

'First I protest publicly, as I have done elsewhere, that I propose and wish with all my heart with the help of God's grace, to be a wholehearted Christian, and as long as breath remains in me, to put forward and defend the law of Christ as well as I can,' he wrote in a tract called 'Declarationes'[4]. He thought, perhaps naively, that if he could help folks understand properly what he was trying to say then they would see the truth for themselves and stop accusing him of being a false teacher.

The Pope in Avignon heard the news of Courtenay's and Sudbury's failure at the riotous scene at St Paul's Cathedral in London. Feeling that his clergy had failed him, it was now up to him to show that he would not allow a rebellious priest like John Wycliffe to keep on writing and preaching in this way. As far as Pope Gregory XI was concerned, John was a heretic who was more loyal to the realm of England than he was to the Roman Church.

---

4. **Declarationes** is a Latin word that means Declaration.

On 22nd May 1377, Pope Gregory XI sent three papal 'bulls'[5] to England in which he chastised the church in England for allowing such 'heresy' to spring up in their country. He encouraged the clergy to make every effort to silence John Wycliffe. He sent the first 'bull' to the Archbishop of Canterbury, Simon Sudbury and to the Bishop of London, William Courtenay. The second 'bull' was sent to King Edward III and the third went to the University of Oxford. At the very least, the Pope wanted Wycliffe to be locked up in prison while the authorities looked for more evidence of Wycliffe's false teaching.

While the papal rulings were on their way to England, the members of parliament continued to show that they had every confidence in Dr Wycliffe. One way they demonstrated that was by asking him a question that needed further clarity. They wondered if it was possible for the king to hold on to the treasure of the kingdom for its defence. They obviously did not want any money to go to foreign nations, even if the Pope himself was demanding it. To couch the question spiritually, was it possible for England to stand up to the Pope and disobey his demands without being sinful?

Parliament needed assurance from Wycliffe that it was possible. The government was angry that on previous occasions money that was needed to continue the war against the French was going to a pope who

---

5. A *papal bull* is a ruling on something or someone from the Pope.

lived in France and who supported the enemy of England.

Wycliffe was happy to oblige parliament with a brief and clear reply to their question. As far as he could discern from Scripture, the money belonged to England and should be used for the defence of the realm. If the response from the papists was to remind England that Pope Gregory XI was God's vice-regent and supreme ruler of all kingdoms in Christendom, then England should ask, 'Who gave him this power?' Wycliffe did not find the Pope's claim supported in the Bible. The money that England gave to the papacy should not be treated as a tribute, but as alms for the poor. And the Pope could not demand alms unless there was a genuine need. The papacy was not poor. John always believed that Christ did not intend his church to be wealthy. So let charity begin at home. It would be unwise to send alms from England when the realm needed them urgently.

While John's views made him popular with parliament, it lowered his popularity with the church. Nonetheless, John continued to lead his country forward in the power struggle with the Church of Rome.

The Lambeth Trial

King Edward III died on 21st June 1377 at the age of sixty-five. There were only two people present at his bedside in Sheen Palace when the king took his last breath: the priest who administered the last rites[1], and Alice Perrers who was a mistress[2] of the ageing king. She waited until the priest left the king's bedchamber then robbed the corpse of its jewellery, pulling the king's rings off his fingers. She had been banished from England by the 'Good Parliament' but returned to be at the king's bedside during his final days on earth.

The monarch had been married to Philippa of Hainault for forty years. She gave him twelve children during their marriage: seven sons and five girls. Edward, the Prince of Wales, who was also known as 'The Black Prince', was to be heir to the throne of

---

1. *The Last Rites* are a selection of prayers and sacraments given by a Roman Catholic priest to a person who is in grave danger of dying.

2. *Mistress:* this is a name sometimes given to women who act as though they are a man's wife but aren't married to him. Throughout history kings often had more than one wife, or they had a wife and a mistress, or a wife and other women who were called concubines or slaves. Each of these scenarios goes against Exodus 20:14 and Matthew 5:27-29

England. However he died a year earlier after a long and lingering illness on 8th June 1376. Prince Edward was only forty six years old when he died. He was buried in Canterbury Cathedral. Prince Edward's only surviving son, Richard, was now next in line to rule England.

The day before his coronation as king, the young Richard rode on the back of a majestic horse through London, travelling from the Tower to Westminster. It was a magnificent procession of the monarchy, on show for the people of London. The next day, 16th July 1377, Richard was led by his uncle, John of Gaunt, to Westminster Abbey. Richard swore his coronation oath to preserve peace in his realm and to protect the church. He would keep good laws and get rid of bad ones. He would also rule his subjects with justice. The Archbishop of Canterbury anointed Richard with oil and laid the crown upon his head. Then the archbishop put the royal ring upon Richard's finger and placed the sceptre, a symbol of good kingly rule, into the new king's hands. Richard was enthroned in the coronation chair and all the nobles of the land paid homage to him. The new king was only ten years old. He was so tired after the proceedings that he had to be carried back to his palace.

When the Pope signed the papal bulls and dispatched them to England, King Edward III was still alive. By the time the papal bulls reached England, the boy Richard was the new king of the realm.

The Pope realised that Wycliffe would not be silenced if there was no support from the English monarch and his government. Therefore the Pope appealed to the young king and his parliament to back him in his attempts to stop Wycliffe from making any further proclamations against the Church of Rome.

The papal ruling that was sent by the Pope to King Edward III back in May was while the lengthy celebrations of the new king went ahead. When these died down and parliament met again in the autumn of 1377, they renewed the policy of the 'Good Parliament' to take a stand once more against the papacy.

The papal ruling that went to Oxford expressed the Pope's disappointment with the scholars for allowing Dr Wycliffe to continue with his 'false teaching' and to walk freely among them. The Pope threatened to remove the university's privileges that allowed them to teach Scripture and defend the faith of the Roman Catholic Church. The Pope expected the university to quash Dr Wycliffe's teaching and hand him over to the Archbishop of Canterbury and the Bishop of London for trial. The reply from Oxford was not what Pope Gregory XI wanted to hear. The university academics said that they could not imprison 'a man of the King of England' on the orders of the Pope. They had no power to act in the way that the Pope wanted them to, especially when their allegiance and duty to the king went against the Pope's orders.

However, the papal ruling which reached the bishops was acted upon immediately. On receiving a copy of the Pope's ruling, the Bishop of London,

William Courtenay travelled quickly to Lambeth Palace, which was the London residence of the Archbishop of Canterbury, Simon Sudbury.

The archbishop was taking a walk in the palace garden when Courtenay arrived.

'Have you seen this?' Courtenay exclaimed excitedly, waving the papal bull in his right hand as he walked briskly across the lawn to where Sudbury was standing. 'Have you seen this?' he repeated as he came to a stop next to the archbishop.

'Yes. I have seen it, Bishop William,' replied Sudbury coolly.

'We have him this time!' cried Courtenay. 'Haven't we, Archbishop?'

'Come and take a walk with me, William,' said Sudbury. As the two men strolled in the garden, Sudbury continued. 'We must proceed with due caution, William.'

'Your Grace, we have the full support of the Pope to arrest John Wycliffe and bring him to heel,' spat Courtenay.

'John Wycliffe still has many friends in London,' Sudbury said.

'Your Grace, I feel I must remind you that this man's teaching undermines the spiritual authority of the church.'

'You need not remind me of that, William. I am well aware of his dangerous proclamations.'

'Now that the Holy Father has returned from Avignon to the Vatican in Rome, I knew it was only a matter of time before he would take further action to suppress this ... this scoundrel.'

'William, you need to calm down,' Sudbury suggested.

'Forgive me, Your Grace. I have no respect for this man. He is nothing but trouble,' Courtenay said.

'I agree he is trouble,' said Sudbury affirmingly. He looked at the papal bull in Courtenay's grasp. 'The parchment you hold in your hand may make the faithful tremble in Rome. But England is a long way from Rome. The barons could toss this to one side if they wanted to.'

'They would not dare,' said Courtenay.

'They might, if we do not handle this properly,' replied Sudbury. He stopped walking and turned to face Courtenay. 'I do not want a repeat of our last encounter with Professor Wycliffe,' said Sudbury, referring to the trial at St Paul's Cathedral in London a few years before.

'Nor do I, Your Grace,' agreed Courtenay. 'Wycliffe remained silent through the whole affair. As did you, if I remember rightly.'

Sudbury rebuked Courtenay sharply. 'Remember to whom you are speaking. I am not one of your subordinates.'

Although he was known for having a bad temper, Courtenay thought it prudent to hold his tongue. He calmly asked, 'What do you have in mind, Your Grace?' They started walking again.

'I shall call Dr Wycliffe to appear before me here, in Lambeth Palace,' replied Sudbury. 'I shall gather a court of bishops to hear him defend his erroneous teaching or recant of it. Of course, your presence will be required, Bishop William.'

'I am humbly at your service,' replied Courtenay. He was delighted to have his day in court with Dr Wycliffe again. Courtenay thought John would get his comeuppance this time.

Once again, John was summonsed to appear before the Archbishop of Canterbury and his prelates at Lambeth Palace during the month of April 1378. He was not accompanied by any nobles or high ranking government officials this time. Yet John knew that the Lord would give him strength and courage to stand before his accusers and answer them as clearly as he could. The prelates had sent John a list of heresies that they believed he had taught openly against the Church of Rome. He was standing trial for these errors. Receiving the list of charges before the date of the trial at Lambeth gave John the opportunity to prepare some answers to the accusations against him. Once again, he was ready to stand against the might of the Roman papacy.

John walked confidently into the chapel at Lambeth Palace, his black academic gown flowing behind him with each stride. His long dark beard and sombre appearance was in stark contrast to the vibrant silver and gold robes worn by the clergy. The bishops were adorned in lush purple garments. They all stiffened as Wycliffe entered the room. His accusers were ready for a fight, and they planned on winning this time.

A crowd gathered around the palace. Their shouts of support for Wycliffe were unsettling to the lavish council. The crowd followed Wycliffe into the chapel, making plain their sympathies for the accused.

As he stood before the Archbishop of Canterbury, John handed him a parchment. It was his response to the court's accusations against him. He repeated his claim that the Pope had no political authority, but only spiritual authority. He reminded his judges that God was the judge of every man, including the Pope, who could fall into sin like any other person. And like any other person, the Pope should be rebuked for his sin too. Wycliffe stated that priests had no power to forgive people for their sins unless God had forgiven the sinner first of all. The papal threat of excommunicating someone from the Church of Rome was powerless to hurt anyone unless that person had already excommunicated himself or herself from God by sin, which was a more serious and terrible situation to be in for the sinner.

The archbishop did not read John's response when it was handed to him. They were preoccupied with how they might disperse the unwelcomed mob from the chapel. Suddenly a nobleman entered the chapel with a message from the queen mother, Joan of Kent. She was the widow of the Black Prince and mother of

Richard, King of England. She had met Dr Wycliffe in the past and liked him and was prepared to interfere in the proceedings on his behalf.

The nobleman made his presence known to the archbishop and his judges. A hush descended upon the whole gathering. The announcement was then made that the queen mother did not permit the bishops to pass sentence upon Dr Wycliffe! Although the queen mother was prepared to allow the trial to take place, whatever the outcome determined by the court, no action was to be taken against Dr Wycliffe this day.

A loud and deafening cheer of delight rose from the crowd in the chapel. Archbishop Sudbury sank into his seat as if his spine had turned to jelly. Courtenay, the Bishop of London, tried to hide his frustration as best he could, but it was hard for him being a man of bad temperament. His face grew redder and redder with anger. The entire court felt powerless in the face of such high and mighty patronage for John Wycliffe.

From then on, the whole trial was just a farce, and everyone knew it.

Throughout the unfolding drama John remained calm. All the bishops could do was to politely order John to stop teaching those things against the papacy, on account of the scandal which they excited among the laity.

'Just look around at the crowd in the chapel, Dr Wycliffe. The evidence of how easily excitable they are is very clear,' said Sudbury pointing to the jubilant spectators.

Glancing around at the crowd, John could see people from all walks of life there to support him, from the successful and wealthy merchant to the poor London commoner. All of them saw John Wycliffe as a national hero who championed the cause of England against the tyranny of Rome. John made no reply.

'You are permitted to go back to Oxford,' Sudbury announced. Holding up high John's unread reply to the charges against him he shrieked, 'But no more of this!'

Dr Wycliffe turned and walked gracefully out of the chapel. The crowd noisily dispersed behind him. The bishops and clergy sat on, muttering amongst themselves as to how they could make Wycliffe pay for his offences against their church, especially when he was held in such high regard by the nobility of England. John's bold teaching and the inability of the church's hierarchy to reprimand him were making them more resolute to deal decisively with him.

John continued to be committed to teaching the Bible truthfully, clearly, and as helpfully as he could to any who would listen. He firmly believed that the Church of Rome should sit under the authority of the Scriptures and not the other way round. He was not prepared to stop teaching the Bible. He was going to ignore the order to stop doing so.

'I must obey God rather than men,' John said to himself, echoing the words of the apostles when they were dragged before the Jewish ruling council to give account of themselves for proclaiming the name of

Jesus[3]. He knew, however, that the restraint of the court by the queen mother would not be replicated by the pontiff in Rome. John was sure that as soon as the Pope found out about the failure of the court at Lambeth Palace to discipline him, there was bound to be more severe repercussions to follow.

Wycliffe braced himself for further entanglements with the papal authorities. He was not afraid of this. He was convinced that the way for God's church to prosper is when his people hear the Word of God and obey his commands. Jesus said this was the expression of love towards him[4].

No man on earth, not even the Pope himself, was going to stop the 'Evangelical Doctor' proclaim the gospel of Christ. With all his strength, John would keep on calling all people everywhere to repent and follow Christ.

3. Acts 5:29.
4. John 14:15; 1 John 5:1-3.

The Bedside Visit

After everything that had happened in Lambeth Palace, John was resolved to spend as much time as he had left preaching and teaching the Word of God to as many who would listen.

Once safely back in Oxford, John decided to write a second paper in response to the accusations laid against him by the papacy. He was even more courageous in this paper than the one he placed into the hands of his judges in Lambeth Palace. When referring to the Pope, John called him 'Antichrist', or 'Man of Sin', or even 'Lucifer[1]'. He attacked the Church's ruling not to allow ordinary people to read the Bible.

Later John went on to pen another book called, *On The Truth of Holy Scripture*. He contended for the supreme authority and entire sufficiency of the Bible. He argued strongly for the need to translate it into English. For John, the Bible was the ultimate authority in all doctrinal matters. Every Christian in England had the right to study and know the Bible for themselves.

---

1. *Lucifer* is another name for Satan.

Since the Word of God alone was sufficient for salvation, then church law, pilgrimages, fasts, prayers to the saints and even the mass were either unnecessary or unbiblical. A failure to know the Bible would result in a failure to know Christ Jesus. But by faith, he argued, and by asking the Holy Spirit for guidance, a Christian could understand the truth of God. John declared that if you came to a passage that was hard to understand, the fault lay with the reader and not with the Bible.

When John wrote these things, he was seriously considering a translation of the Bible into English. It would be a productive use of time and the skills God had given him as a scholar. For centuries, translations of the Bible in Latin and French were available. But they were expensive and usually they were owned and used by the upper classes of society. John was right to complain that as the gentry of England had the Bible in French[2], the ordinary people of England should have the same words in English.

The 'Evangelical Doctor' was not worried about the consequences of his writings. As a pastor, John knew he must fight the wolves that come in sheep's clothing to steal away the flock of God. He must use 'the sword of the Spirit, which is the Word of God[3]' to defeat the enemy of God's people. He must teach good theology

2. See *Fact File* called 'The Normans' to find out why the gentry of England had French Bibles.
3. Ephesians 6:17

to the men and women of England while there was still breath in his body. God would help him do it.

In the meantime, a huge and important event happened in Rome that distracted John's enemies. Pope Gregory XI, who had issued the papal bulls against John the year before, had died in the spring of 1378. An assembly of sixteen cardinals[4] met in Rome to appoint his successor. Eleven of them were Frenchmen and wanted the new Pope to be French. However, the papal court was now back in Rome. The Roman people did not want it to return to Avignon in France. An agitated crowd gathered around the hall where the cardinals met to discuss whom they would elect. The cardinals were threatened by the crowd who demanded they appoint a Roman person as the next Pope. If they didn't, then none of the cardinals would leave the building alive. The cardinals gave in to the crowd's demands, and they unanimously elected the Archbishop of Bari as the new Pope. He became known as Pope Urban VI.

Wycliffe was hopeful that the new Pope would bring about reform in the church. Pope Urban VI appeared to start well by immediately introducing a wage cut for the cardinals! That was a good sign, as far as John was concerned. The church was too wealthy, and the senior clergy were far too well-off. John always maintained that the Church of Christ was not to be wealthy. Not surprisingly, the change was not welcomed by the

---

4. A *cardinal* is a senior member of the clergy in the Roman Catholic Church.

cardinals. On top of that, Pope Urban VI also had a very different view concerning his power and authority in the Church of Rome. He saw his power as absolute. His cardinals did not share this view. They held a more traditional understanding that it was their responsibility to limit the power and authority of a despotic Pope.

Something had to be done. The French cardinals who were involved in the election of Pope Urban VI met again to come up with a plan. They declared that the election of a Roman Pope was done under extreme pressure from the threatening mob in Rome. Therefore they announced that the election of Pope Urban VI was not valid. Immediately they elected one of their own French cardinals to be the new Pope. They chose Cardinal Robert of Geneva who became Pope Clement VII. He settled his papal court in Avignon in France.

Both popes remained adamant that their election to the highest position in the church was valid. Each claimed to be the 'Vicar of Christ' on earth. Now there were two of them! Pope Urban VI excommunicated Pope Clement VII in Avignon. Pope Clement VII excommunicated Pope Urban VI in Rome. They cursed each other and hurled insults upon each other. The whole debacle of the rival Popes denouncing each other brought a lot of confusion and resulted in a tremendous loss of respect for the papacy around the world[5].

It was clear to John, and he hoped to others, that the entire papal system was at odds with biblical

---

5. **The Great Schism** as it became known was from 1378-1417.

Christianity. It was time to write another book. He called it *The Schism of the Popes* and he invited the rulers of Europe to seize the opportunity to free themselves of all papal control.

'We trust in the help of Christ,' John wrote. 'For Christ has begun already to help us graciously, in that he has divided the head of the Antichrist, and made the two parts fight against each other; for there is no doubt whatsoever that the sin of the Popes, which has continued for so long, has brought about the division.'

The division of the Popes lasted a long time. Unfortunately the rulers of Europe failed to shake off the shackles of papal authority as John had hoped. They opted to choose a Pope and support him. England chose Pope Urban VI in Rome. France supported Pope Clement VII in Avignon. European countries groaned under the weight of papal taxation as they tried to support two rival Popes in two countries. Ordinary people no longer held the papacy in high esteem.

The trial at Lambeth Palace, the strain of opposition, the desire to teach the people of England as much biblical truth as possible, and the fact that he was getting on in years, were all starting to take their toll on John.

In 1379, while he was still at Oxford, John became seriously ill. His enemies, especially the friars, were overjoyed to hear the news of John's weakened health. They thought John was going to die and wondered if he might recant his teaching against the Roman Church before that happened. Representatives from the friaries, along with four city officials, decided to pay John a visit at his residence in Queen's College, Oxford.

A loud knock came to the door. It was answered by a servant who was attending to John as he lay ill in bed. John heard the knock and wondered who it might be. Perhaps it was Nicholas Hereford calling to pray with him. Imagine his surprise when his room was filled with people who secretly rejoiced in his demise and wanted him to recant of his teaching against the wicked practices of the Church of Rome!

The men gathered around John's bedside and peered down at him as he lay on his back.

'My good Dr Wycliffe how are you feeling?' asked one of the friars, feigning concern for his wellbeing.

Before he was able to reply, another friar spoke to him. 'When we heard of your serious ailment, we thought it best to come and see you.'

'Indeed,' said another. 'We are praying for your restoration.' John found that difficult to believe. Yet he played along and nodded appreciatively.

There was a moment's silence, then the visitors tone changed.

'You have death on your lips,' said a stout friar. 'Be moved by your faults and retract in our presence all that you have said that has hurt us.'

'If you do not recant of these false teachings against us,' interjected another friar, 'you will face the wrath and judgement of heaven!'

'There it is, the real reason for their visit,' thought John. It was now obvious that this visit was not to wish John a speedy recovery from his illness. Rather their motivation was to get him to recant of the grievous wrongs they felt he had committed against them.

The ailing Wycliffe said nothing in response for the moment. He looked at his servant and in a quiet voice asked for his help to raise him a little on his pillow. The servant obliged and gently helped John sit up in bed. He was very weak and could hardly support himself. The servant remained at his side to give him extra assistance.

One by one John looked at the serious faces of the friars and officials around him. Then in a strong voice he declared, 'I shall not die but live and again declare the evil deeds of the friars!'

They were astonished at his words. They huffed and tutted and moaned loudly. Then they left his bedside, rushing out of the room in a state of confusion. 'Did Dr Wycliffe really believe that he would recover and make more trouble for them?' they wondered. 'He looked like he was a death's door. Surely not? Hopefully not!'

When the unwelcomed visitors left, John sank slowly into his bed. His servant helped ease him into a comfortable position and fixed his pillow. The encounter took it out of him, although their reaction to his rebuff was quite amusing. John wanted to get well. There was still important gospel work for him to do.

Lying in his sickbed, John prayed quietly, asking the Lord to restore him to health and allow him the strength to keep contending for the true faith of Christ in England. The people needed an English translation of the Bible to help them know Christ and serve him all their days. The people also needed to hear clear and simple gospel preaching that would encourage them to repent and believe in Jesus Christ personally. He begged the Lord to raise up men for this vital work in England.

The Lord graciously laid his healing hand upon John and restored him to health. In thankfulness of heart, he devoted the remaining years of his life to the vital tasks of making good Bible teaching available for all who wanted it. Not only that, but he would also help provide an English translation of the Bible. And if the good Lord saw fit to give him the strength, he would train and deploy preachers of the gospel of Christ throughout the nation of England.

Dr Wycliffe was under no illusion – this important work would set him on a collision course with the Church of Rome again.

The English Bible

The lecture hall in the Augustinian Friary just off Cat Street in Oxford was brimming with students eager to hear Dr Wycliffe speak against the teachings and practices of the Roman Church. For a while now he had been lecturing about the importance of the Lord's Supper[1]. The Roman Church taught that during the mass, as they called it, the priest had the power with his words to change the bread and wine into the real body and blood of Christ. This doctrine, known as 'Transubstantiation[2]' was a crucial teaching of the church and one that John was prepared to challenge. He condemned it as idol-worship and said the idea that a priest had the power to change bread and wine into the very flesh and blood of Christ was supremely arrogant.

---

1. The early church had observed this practice as described in the Gospels and in 1 Corinthians 11, according to Christ's declaration, 'Do this in remembrance of me.' Read Matthew 26:26-29; Mark 14:22-25; Luke 22:14-20; 1 Corinthians 11:23-29.

2. *Transubstantiation* means *a change of substance*. In other words, the bread completely changes into the flesh of Christ, and the wine completely changes into the blood of Christ. Go to the *Fact File* called 'Transubstantiation' at the back of the book for more information.

'Transubstantiation cannot be shown to have any foundation in the Word of God,' he declared to his students. It was a blatant disregard for the church's teaching on the Eucharist and it caused the students to murmur amongst themselves. John allowed the statement to sink in and waited for the hall to quieten down before adding, 'Transubstantiation is a blasphemous deceit.' Some students tutted while others groaned. There was another moment's pause to regain silence. Then John added, 'No pilgrim on earth is able to see Christ in the consecrated host[3] with the bodily eye, but by faith.' His voice was clear and firm.

Some students displayed an admiration for the courage of Dr Wycliffe to speak against the foundational teachings of the church. Others were not so enamoured with his reformed conclusions. The friars were furious when they heard what Dr Wycliffe was saying about the Eucharist.

When John wrote a treatise called 'On The Eucharist' in the spring of 1381, the church was shaken to its core. Within the document, John sought to encourage debate with those who disagreed with his conclusions about the doctrine of transubstantiation. No one was prepared to take up the gauntlet thrown down by the professor. Instead, the church hierarchy branded Dr Wycliffe a 'heretic'

---

3. The **consecrated host** means that the bread and wine on the table has been set apart as holy.

because he denounced the teachings of the Church of Rome.

The Chancellor of Oxford University, William de Berton, called a secret meeting of a council to come up with a suitable course of action against him. The council was made up of twelve doctors, eight of whom were monks or friars. During the meeting they described John's views of the Eucharist as full of error and opposed to the decisions of the church.

The council decided that John was to stop teaching his opinions on the Eucharist. If he refused, he would face excommunication from the university, suspension, and imprisonment. In fact, anyone who taught or even listened to John's teaching concerning transubstantiation would be disciplined in a similar manner by the university.

Dr Wycliffe did not know about the decision against him until a short while later, when he was interrupted during another lecture on the Lord's Supper. He could see a messenger of the university walk towards him with a scroll in his hand. John imagined it was an important note and stopped what he was saying in order to receive it from the messenger's grasp. Instead, the messenger stopped before Dr Wycliffe, unrolled the scroll, and began to read out the sentence that had been passed down by the secret council.

'Dr Wycliffe, by order of the Chancellor and council of the University of Oxford, from this time forward you are to stop teaching your erroneous views on the subject of transubstantiation. And should you, or any other member of the university fail to comply with this order and continue to teach your erroneous views in the schools and elsewhere, you shall be excommunicated, suspended from all teaching exercises, and imprisoned. This punishment shall also apply to those who listen to your opinions on this matter.'

The students watching the event unfold before them were stunned. This was nothing less than Dr Wycliffe's expulsion from his beloved Oxford. John was hesitant for a moment, too, as he thought carefully about his next words and actions. What should he do? Obey men and save his life? But surely that would dishonour God? His mind quickly raced to the apostles who were hauled in before the religious council in Jerusalem and ordered not to speak about Jesus anymore. Wycliffe knew what he must do. With God's help, he would stand firm.

'But you ought first to have shown me that I am in error,' Wycliffe said to the messenger. He simply wanted to debate these things with anyone in the university who was willing to do so. Instead he was condemned by the council without any discussion on the matter. The messenger simply repeated the sentence on the scroll.

'Then I appeal to the king and to parliament,' replied John. 'Take my reply back to the chancellor and his council.'

The messenger left the silent hall. The students were dismissed for the day. Wycliffe returned to his room at Queen's. Barely had he closed the door when he heard someone knocking on it. It was John Purvey, a young but brilliant scholar who had become a friend to Wycliffe in recent years. Purvey was accompanied by Nicholas Hereford.

'Dr Wycliffe, please forgive our intrusion,' said Purvey.

'It is always good to see you both. Please come in.'

Purvey and Hereford entered and stood in the centre of the room as John closed the door behind them.

'What can I do for you?' John asked.

'I heard that you received a visit from a university messenger today, Dr Wycliffe. Is it true what they say?' Purvey asked.

'Ah, indeed it is. Tell me what you heard, John.'

'Only that you have been forbidden to teach the truth about the Eucharist.'

'Yes. I am afraid that is correct.'

'What will you do?' asked Nicholas.

'I shall continue to teach the Word of God in all its glorious splendour.'

The men were relieved. A great amount of pressure from church authorities had been brought to bear on Dr Wycliffe over the years for his faithful teaching of the Word of God, but he had never lost the favour of the university until now. It seemed that his time at Oxford was coming to an end. Yet John was still defiant of ecclesiastical bullies and despotic popes who sought to malign the truth of Scripture for their own powerful gains.

'We must stand our ground in the face of sinful opposition, gentlemen, and echo the words of the psalmist:

> 'I love you, O LORD, my strength.
> The LORD is my rock and my
> fortress and my deliverer,
> my God, my rock in whom I take refuge,
> my shield, and the horn of my
> salvation, my stronghold.
> I call upon the LORD, who is
> worthy to be praised,
> and I am saved from my enemies[4]."

'Amen, Dr Wycliffe!' exclaimed Purvey. He often found being in the company of Dr Wycliffe inspiring.

'Thank you for coming to see me. I am alright. Do not worry. Trust in the Lord. And pray for our enemies, that the Lord in his grace would open their eyes to see the error of their ways,' John said. 'Take a seat. I have something that I want to ask you both.'

Hereford perched at the end of the bed while Purvey took the seat in the corner of the room.

'I believe it is time for a translation of the Bible into English and I was wondering if you would help me achieve it?'

---

4. Psalm 18:1-3.

'I have known for a while now that this was close to your heart, John.' said Nicholas.

'That is true, Nicholas. I have been working on this idea since the summer last year,' said John, 'along with developing an order of preachers who will take the simple gospel to the people of England.' He looked at Purvey and continued. 'My reason for the Bible in English is very simple. Christ and his apostles taught the people in the language best known to them. It is certain that the Christian faith becomes more evident the more the gospel itself is known. Therefore, the doctrine should not only be in Latin but in the common tongue.'

John began to pace up and down the room as he spoke. He was giving his reasons for having the Bible in English. Both men had heard them before over the years, but always found it helpful to have the good Dr Wycliffe remind them.

'The laity ought to understand the faith. The doctrines of our faith are in the Scriptures. If it is heresy to read the Bible, then the Holy Spirit himself is condemned. He gave the appropriate tongues to the apostles of Christ, to enable them to speak the Word of God in all languages that were ordained under heaven[5]. If you deny Christ's words as heresy, then you make Christ a heretic. If you condemn the Word of God in any language as heresy, then you condemn God for being a heretic

---

5. Acts 2:1-41.

that spoke the word, because God and his Word are one. If his Word is the life of the world, how can any false teacher take it away from those of us who are Christian men and women and allow the people to die for hunger of the truth?'

'I am with you, Dr Wycliffe!' declared Purvey as he quickly jumped to his feet.

'As am I,' added Nicholas.

John smiled. 'Wonderful, wonderful,' he said gleefully, and shook the men's hands as a sign of their agreement. 'We shall begin this task soon.'

When Hereford and Purvey left, John knelt by his bed and prayed to the Lord for strength and wisdom in the days ahead. Deep down he felt that there may not be much support for him from government this time. He was not defending the realm against paying those outrageous taxations demanded by a greedy papacy. He was challenging the flawed foundations of the church's teaching on the Eucharist. But he was thrilled to have the support of his younger Christian friends in the vital task of Bible translation. He gave thanks to God for such encouragement.

A few days after the debacle in the lecture hall, John received an unexpected visitor. His patron, John of Gaunt, hurried to Oxford to speak with him. He was dismayed that John was attacking the church's teaching about the Eucharist. He was also aware of the sentence that was delivered against John from the Chancellor of Oxford University.

Dr Wycliffe spent time explaining the problem to his patron. But in the end, John of Gaunt advised his protégé to stop teaching and writing about the Eucharist. 'It is for your own good,' Gaunt said.

'I cannot remain silent when the Antichrist and his minions are at work in the world,' John said.

'The king and his parliament are unlikely to support you in this matter. Do you realise this?'

'So be it,' replied John. 'I have the support of God and his Word. That is enough for me, as it should be for you.'

'There will be no return from this, Dr Wycliffe. No one will be by your side this time, not even me. Be reasonable. Remain silent on this matter.'

'I am being reasonable,' said John. 'I wanted a public debate on this issue. But I was met with unreasonable antagonism instead. I am afraid I will not be silent. I cannot allow the falsehoods to go unchecked by the Word of God. It is out of the question that I remain silent.'

Both men stared at each other and said nothing for a moment. Then Gaunt suggested,

'Perhaps it would be wise for you to withdraw to your parish at Lutterworth. The university can do nothing to you there.'

John said nothing. Gaunt left him to reflect on his advice and returned to London. He was completely bewildered by the stance his protégé had taken. It was difficult for him to believe that Wycliffe would willingly relinquish the support given to him in the past from his monarch, his government, and himself.

Dr Wycliffe knew that he would be alone the moment he confronted Rome's bad theology on the Eucharist. It seemed that everyone in England believed what the church said about it. No one had dared challenge that before because not many could read the Bible for themselves in their own language. Only a small percentage of the population of England understood Latin. People simply believed what the Church of Rome told them.

If ever there was a need for an English Bible for all the people, and for clear gospel preachers throughout England, it was now.

The Bible Men

Lutterworth in Leicestershire, England, became the training centre of Wycliffe's 'Bible Men'. This venture started when he was in Oxford. Some students who were training to be clergy and who were in sympathy with Dr Wycliffe's Bible teaching, sought training and opportunities for practical preaching experience from him. But after John had effectively been ousted from Oxford by the authorities, the training for his itinerant preachers continued in his parish of Lutterworth.

They were also called 'Poor Priests' not because the standard of their preaching was poor, but because they were itinerant preachers who had no income. They set off with wooden staffs in their hands. They were poorly dressed in robes made from rough material. They lived on the charity of the communities where they taught the Word of God, eating the simplest types of food given to them. In these things, there was a similarity with the begging friars. However, John warned his 'Bible Men' not to be like the friars that he rebuked so severely in the past.

A group of preachers descended upon Lutterworth for the important task of proclaiming the Word of God to all the lost souls in England. The men were expecting John to instruct them how they might preach the gospel clearly and helpfully to anyone who was willing to hear them. They wanted to learn from John's example as he preached from the pulpit in St Mary's.

One day, a small group of preachers walked into the rectory at Lutterworth, including John Aston, Nicholas Hereford, Philip Repton, Robert Arlington, and John Ashwardby. These men were once leading men of Oxford. Now they were part of John's band of 'Bible Men'. He greeted them warmly at the front door as they filed into the sitting room. On their way in to the rectory, John Purvey provided every preacher with some portions of Scripture. These had been translated into English by Dr Wycliffe's small group of Oxford translators who had also followed him to Lutterworth. The task had taken them quite some time but their aim was a full translation of the Bible into English.

As they entered the sitting room, some of the men sat on chairs, while others found a wall to stand against. Once settled into the room, they waited eagerly to hear from John, in preparation for their mission to win the nation of England for Christ.

John made his way through the group to the unlit hearth. He turned to look at his 'Poor Priests'. He started every preachers' meeting with prayer. John begged the Lord to help them in the task of gospel proclamation and to equip each of them with the skill to teach the Bible well and with courage. A loud 'Amen' echoed throughout the room.

'Some men tell tales that they find in the lives of the saints outside the Holy Scriptures,' he began. 'This sort of thing often pleases the people very much. But we hold to a better way – to leave such empty words and trust in God. We speak of his law and especially his Gospels.' John held up his copy of the Scriptures and continued, 'And, since these words are God's words, they should be taken as believed, and they will give people life, new life, more than other words.'

John looked to the heavens and erupted into spontaneous prayer. 'We praise you, O Lord Christ!' he cried out, 'whose divine power overpowers strong men in arms, softens hard hearts, and renews and changes them into godly men; men who had been brutalized by sins, and who had departed infinitely far from God.'

His eyes dropped to look at the faces of the men before him. 'Obviously such miraculous power could never be worked by the word of a priest, if the Spirit of Life and the Eternal Word, did not, above everything else, work with it,' he said. His tone became stern as he warned the men that the power to convert someone from spiritual death to spiritual life did not rest on their powers of persuasion. 'It is not you who preach,' John said pointing a finger at them, 'but the Spirit of the Father which speaks in you and since the works of the

Trinity are inseparable, it is Trinity which speaks. The gospel of Christ must be preached to the people as God commands.'

'Dr Wycliffe, what if they do not appear interested in listening to us?' asked Repton. 'Do we change our method to entice them to hear us?'

'I once overheard two students at Merton talking about the method of preaching,' interrupted Aston. 'One said to the other that 'the Bible should never get in the way of a good story.' I hoped he was joking, but sadly I am not certain he was!'

'Do not trouble yourself about any new fashion of preaching which may arise,' John replied. 'The only care must be how to be useful as far as possible to the people. The truth must be proclaimed to them even though they may receive it unwillingly,' he continued. 'We do not tell them comedies or tragedies, nor do we tell them fables or droll stories, but simply and solely the Law of the Lord as Christ and the apostles delivered it. For in the gospel is hidden the life which is able to enliven the church.'

These words were so important for the preachers to hear from Dr Wycliffe. The people of England were familiar with religious entertainment that masqueraded as 'preaching'. The friars loved to talk about the legends of saints, or tell tragic stories, or recite poems, or relay coarse comedies filled with unwholesome illustrations, all in the name of 'preaching'. A favourite was the interpretations of dreams. If it held the attention of their listeners, then there was no story that was too ridiculous for the friars to tell. Dr Wycliffe did not want his 'Bible Men' to be anything like the itinerant friars of the nation.

'If your soul is not in harmony with your words, how can the words have power?' asked John rhetorically. 'If there is no love in your heart for the people, you are just a sounding brass and a tinkling symbol,' he added, resonating the words of the apostle Paul in 1 Corinthians 13.

'The Lord's Word is the food which sustains the church,' he said. 'The preacher who preaches to the people without reading the gospel and clearly explaining it to them, gives the people a meal without bread. Those sham bishops set aside the gospel. If they mention the gospel at all, they do not preach it in full.'

John left no doubt in the minds of the men in the room that the Bible had to be central in preaching. He strongly criticized those who were guilty of not preaching the Word of God. It wasn't that the Bible was not used in the sermon - it was usual for a preacher to read out a Bible passage. The problem lay in what happened next. They would take the main contents of their sermons from other sources and not teach the Bible passage itself.

'The sermon should be pointed, but not bitter,' said John. 'Therefore, go and preach, it is the most wonderful work,' John exhorted the men. 'But do not imitate the priests who go to the pub after the sermon and drink too much beer or sit gambling at the gaming table. Men, when your sermon is over, go and visit the sick, the aged, the poor, the blind and the lame. Comfort them.

Jesus Christ himself spoke God's words anywhere that he knew they might be of great benefit to the people who heard them. The Lord often preached at dinner or supper times – whenever it was convenient for others to hear him. You do the same.'

Conscious of the vital need of the Holy Spirit in every work of ministry, John prayed for strength and courage in the task of proclaiming Christ to a world steeped in darkness.

'Men, let us pray.' The preachers got on their knees as John led them in prayer.

'Almighty Lord God, by your Holy Spirit, you made the apostles so strong that they were not afraid of any man, nor of pain, nor death. Help us, your poor servants, by the gifts of the same Holy Spirit, to be strong, and bold in your cause to maintain the gospel against Antichrist and the tyrants of this world. Amen.'

As they got up to leave, John gave them some parting words of wisdom. 'Remember, gentlemen. Christ's church does not need clever graduates who are promoted to rich parishes, but simple men following Christ and his doctrine.'

Dr Wycliffe believed that his 'Bible Men' should move about the country and not settle in any one place for long. He expected the preachers to give themselves to serious Bible study too. Many people saw John Aston, Nicholas Hereford and the other 'Poor Priests' from Oxford wandering the heaths and roads of the land.

If a local church did not welcome them into the pulpit, the 'Bible Men' preached in the graveyards. They preached in people's homes. They spoke to a few folk at a time, and to large crowds in the villages and towns all over England. They preached to the nobility and they preached to the common folk. Wherever anyone was willing to listen, they spoke the Word of God to them. They pointed people to Christ Jesus and the salvation that he offers through his cross. Many people believed and were saved. They increased in number so much that their enemies began to complain as it seemed that every second person on the street was a Lollard[1].

When the preachers returned to Lutterworth, they told John all about their experiences on the road. The one thing that was clear to John when he heard their stories was the need for a full Bible translation in the English language that could be made available to everyone. All his preachers could do was teach the people of England short passages of Scripture to memorise. Yet he kept hearing a consistent message from them – the people were eager to hear the Word of God.

The authorities of the church did everything to try and wipe Wycliffe's preachers from the face of the earth. The friars hated them. They joined forces with the other clergy of England in expressing their hostility to the 'Bible Men'.

It pained John to hear tales of opposition to the cause of the gospel from his preachers. Nicholas Hereford had

---

1. A *Lollard* was the term given to followers of John Wycliffe because of their alleged muttering. The word is thought to mean 'mutter' or 'mumble' in the Dutch language.

returned to Lutterworth from one of his walk-abouts. He met John at the rectory and began to tell him all about his journey to some of the local towns and villages.

'On one occasion, Dr Wycliffe, a friar tried to shout me down as I spoke to a small gathering of people in a village not that far from here,' said Nicholas. 'The friar called me all manner of wicked things; I cannot repeat them. But he was quite vitriolic in his attack. It seemed to me that his main point against my presence there was that I did not have the permission of the bishop to speak to the people!' he exclaimed.

This came as no surprise to John. 'Worldly bishops demand that no one preach the gospel, Nicholas, except according to their wills and the limits they place upon the ministers to do so,' he said. 'The bishops do not allow people to hear the gospel. But since it is the counsel and commandment of Christ to his ministers that they preach the gospel, they must do it without the permission of the bishops, who are fiends of hell. Sadly, it seems that priests may not obey the commands of Jesus Christ unless they have the permission of these fiends.'

John closed his eyes to pray, and Nicholas quickly bowed his head. 'Lord Jesus,' he prayed, 'are these sinful fools and in some cases fiends of hell, more clever and mighty than you, that true Christian men may not do your will, unless they have their permission?'

He paused briefly and took a deep breath.

'Merciful Lord,' he sighed, 'you are all wise and full of love. How long will you put up with these Antichrists that hate you and your holy gospel, and prevent the good health of the souls of men? But I pray that you will help these poor and wretched men, that they may come to possess the love and reverence for your gospel. I pray that they may not be hindered to worship you and to do your will because of these false teachings of the devil.'

'Amen,' said Nicholas softly.

John opened his eyes slowly. 'Time for supper, I think,' he said.

The Earthquake Synod

After the Black Death killed over a third of the population in England[1], there was a great shortage of people to work the land. Many peasants, labourers and smallholders were able to secure higher wages. But there were more wars and the cost of maintaining armies soared. As a result, people had to pay additional taxes. The government introduced a Poll Tax of one shilling[2] that it expected the citizens of England to pay. It was a week's wages for a skilled labourer. Many peasants lived in great poverty. They had little to eat, and survived on porridge, bread and vegetables, with a little fish or meat occasionally. So they protested against their austere existence. They wanted an end to serfdom[3] and better labour conditions. About sixty thousand men from the English counties of Kent and

---

1. England had a population of 5-6 million people at the time of the Black Death in the fourteenth century. So it is estimated that around 2 million people died as a result of the plague.
2. A *shilling* was about twelve British pence in medieval England.
3. In medieval times, *a serf* was a tenant farmer whose life was bound to a plot of land owned by a landlord. A *serf* was expected to work hard, pay rent and obey the will of his landlord.

Essex descended upon London, burning castles, and killing officials and lawyers on their way.

On 13th June 1381 the rioters entered the City of London and surrounded the Tower, where the king, his mother, some noblemen and the Archbishop of Canterbury were sheltering. The next day, the king went to negotiate with the rebels at a location three miles away from the tower. King Richard promised them everything that they demanded. However, while he was away from the Tower, some rebels broke in and murdered the Archbishop of Canterbury, William Sudbury, by cutting off his head. They wounded one of the noblemen who was the king's cousin in that attack too.

As the king was on his way back to the Tower the following day, he was waylaid by the rebel army at Smithfield in London. Their leader, Wat Tyler, rode up to King Richard and made further demands in a rude and menacing manner. The Lord Mayor of London was accompanying the king on his journey. Outraged by Tyler's threatening demeanour, the mayor stabbed him, killing Tyler immediately.

When the rebels saw that their chief was dead, they planned to advance on the king and his entourage to murder all of them. But the fourteen-year-old king rode over to them and cried out in a loud voice, 'Sirs, would you kill your king? I am your king. I am your captain and your leader.' He made promises to address their demands. Then the rebels dispersed, satisfied that the king would champion their cause.

King Richard's bravery saved his own life and the lives of his followers. Parliament, however, did not honour any of the king's promises to the people.

Incredibly, John Wycliffe was blamed for 'The Peasants Revolt' as it became known. Some troublemakers pointed to the things that John said over the years that led people to believe that any institution could be challenged, no matter how established it was. John always encouraged people to think for themselves, which didn't go down too well with the privileged of society.

The 'Bible Men' were falsely accused of stoking the fire of rebellion among the population. They were blamed for encouraging the serfs to challenge the right of the landowners to be their overlords.

None of it was true. The 'Bible Men' were never known to show hostility to any landowner. In fact, they cultivated good relationships with the landed gentry and were often welcomed into their homes to talk about the gospel with them.

It was not surprising that the revolt was seized upon by John's enemies to accuse him of being the instigator of the riots. It was a cunning and wicked ploy to sully John's name and frighten the authorities into thinking that he was a powerful enemy. But it was all a fabrication. John had nothing to do with the revolt. No one could bring any charge against him to say otherwise. The rumour, however, was enough to encourage John to stay in his parish in Lutterworth.

The vacancy in Lambeth Palace that was created by the Peasants Revolt needed to be filled. In October 1381, the Bishop of London, William Courtenay, was nominated to be the new Archbishop of Canterbury. He was thrilled by his elevation to the top job in the church in England. Courtenay now had the power that he so desperately wanted to deal with his nemesis, John Wycliffe. But he wanted to wait until he received his vestments from Rome. Without these special items of clothing, Courtenay did not feel that he could perform his duties as the Archbishop properly. Once the vestments arrived, Courtenay would be content to start his pursuit of Wycliffe, knowing he had full papal authority to go after him.

In the meantime, John suffered a mild stroke from the immense strain that he was under. He was thankful that he was not alone at the rectory. Nicholas Hereford and John Purvey were with him and helped him back to strength. Not long after the downturn in his health, John was starting to get better.

'How are you feeling today?' Purvey asked as he walked over to the rector's bedside.

'Much improved,' replied John.

Purvey opened the curtains to let some light into the room from the morning sunshine. 'I am glad to hear it,' he said.

'I want to get back to the translation work today,' said John.

'Do you feel well enough, Dr Wycliffe?' asked Purvey.

'I do,' said John. 'Will you let Nicholas know?'

'Yes, I will tell him.'

'I will be down shortly,' said John.

As Purvey left the bedroom, John rose from his bed and dressed slowly. He was pleased to be feeling so much better. As he did every morning, John thanked the Lord from the depths of his heart for another new day in which to serve him. John wanted to keep going on the translation of the Latin Bible into English. He needed to finish it despite the prohibitions of the papacy. The men who came to Oxford with him were good scholars. John was very confident that together they could provide the nation with a Bible in their own language.

Downstairs, the table in the dining room was covered in paper. Nicholas and John sat talking quietly about the work that they were doing. When John entered the room they paused their conversation to welcome him.

'Good morning, Dr Wycliffe,' said Nicholas. 'You look better.'

'Good morning, Nicholas. Yes, I feel much better, thank you. Please forgive me for interrupting your conversation.' John sat down next to him.

'Oh, do not worry about that, professor,' said Purvey. 'We were just discussing the work in hand.'

'Yes, it is a very important work,' said John. 'The people of England must be able to read the entire Word of God for themselves. And the good Lord has given us the task of helping them do it.'

The men nodded in agreement. It was common knowledge that John loved the Bible. Purvey and Hereford had full confidence in John's oversight of translating the Word of God into English. Due care and attention was taken with every sentence. The scholars worked long and hard for many months. The Latin was hard to translate smoothly into English at times, but the men did not give up because what they were doing was vital to the spiritual health of the nation.

However, their work was interrupted by the Archbishop of Canterbury, William Courtenay. His episcopal vestments had finally arrived from Rome. Now he felt that his investiture to the See of Canterbury[4] was complete. He could begin his persecution of John Wycliffe.

On 17th May 1382, Courtenay called a synod[5] to meet at Blackfriars Abbey[6] in London. It was a very large council that included eight bishops, twenty academics, four monks and fifteen friars. The way the

---

4. The *See of Canterbury* is another term for the Diocese of Canterbury that covers most of East Kent in England.

5. A *synod* is a council of the church.

6. *Blackfriars Abbey* was the same building that Henry VIII appeared in when he wanted a divorce from Catherine of Aragon. For further reading, see *Thomas Cranmer – The King's Ambassador* in the Trailblazer series.

council was put together implied that John wasn't going to get a fair trial. By now everyone knew that the monks and friars hated him passionately for preaching against them.

Archbishop Courtenay made up a list of 'heresies' that John was supposed to have taught. The top of the list was John's attack on the church's teaching of transubstantiation. Courtenay distributed copies of his list to the council members as they sat down.

All of a sudden, the building began to tremble. A powerful earthquake was shaking the whole city of London. The synod was terrified, thinking that God was angry with them for condemning John Wycliffe and his followers. They hastily got up from their seats and tried to run out of the building. But Courtenay interpreted what was happening in a different way. He bellowed at the fleeing clergy to sit back down. They returned to their seats, nervously looking up to see if anything was about to fall on their heads. When the trembling stopped Courtenay addressed his council to help soothe their fears.

'Do you not know that the deadly vapours which catch fire in the bosom of the earth, and give rise to these phenomena which alarm you, lose all their force when they burst forth?' he said. 'In the same way, by rejecting the wicked from our community, we shall put an end to the convulsions of the church.'

In other words, the trial was still on. Selections of John's writings were read out loud and condemned unanimously as unorthodox and untrue. John was never called to appear before the synod to defend his teaching. However, some of his supporters were, including Nicholas Hereford, who had to interrupt his Bible translation work in order to attend.

When the synod finished, their conclusions were sent to all the bishops in England. The bishops then declared to their clergy that Wycliffe's doctrines were absolutely forbidden. Anyone who supported Wycliffe would be severely disciplined if caught teaching his 'heresies' in the diocese.

The Archbishop of Canterbury was not content to allow Oxford University to get away with tolerating Wycliffe's instruction. Robert Rygge was the Chancellor of the university. Rygge took over from William de Berton earlier that year and he was much more sympathetic to Dr Wycliffe's position than his predecessor. Courtenay realised that he would not get any support from Rygge to rid Oxford of Wycliffe's influence. So, the archbishop appealed to the young King of England in a written correspondence.

In his letter to the king, Courtenay argued that to allow Wycliffe to appeal continually to the passions of the people, the destruction of Church and State was inevitable. He implored the king to help silence the Lollards.

King Richard was persuaded by Courtenay's plea and sided with his archbishop on this issue. Courtenay had the king's authority to imprison the Lollards for upholding the Biblical teachings of Wycliffe. Sadly, many of those who supported John in Oxford began to step back from him for fear of incarceration. Martyrdom was not attractive to them. And while it was believed that John of Gaunt, Wycliffe's former patron, had abandoned him, the Archbishop of Canterbury could not be that sure of Gaunt's support. The memory of the fiasco at St Paul's still lingered in his mind. Gaunt had the reputation of only looking out for himself. Only those people who served Gaunt's purposes received his benefaction.

John's support was dwindling among the nobility of London and the academics of Oxford. He was also in poor health. Yet the fire in his heart, to serve the Lord with gladness and proclaim his saving gospel, burned all the more intensely. Yes, Oxford may now be closed to him, but on the positive side, there were some Oxford men who decided that if the colleges were no longer open to free discussion, then they must flee to Lutterworth. These men gathered around John in his parish, and they strengthened the others who were already training there.

On a beautiful day in 1382 John finally announced to his preachers that the first translation of the Bible in English was completed. There was spontaneous rejoicing as the men gave thanks to the Lord for his grace and mercy in allowing the work to be completed without interference from their enemies.

The Heavenly Call

On 19th November 1382, John walked into the Houses of Parliament in London. The appeal that he made to the king and parliament a while back when he was accused of teaching heresy by the Chancellor of Oxford University was finally being heard.

The chamber was full of important people who were interested to understand what possible reasons John had for attacking the fundamental doctrine of transubstantiation in the Mass.

John stood before the large gathering and began to make his appeal. At first, John called for the members of parliament to consider changing the monastic Orders. He believed the vows that members of the Orders were called upon to make were not natural and enslaved the person making the vows.

'Since Jesus Christ shed his blood to free his church, therefore I demand its freedom,' John said in a strong and clear voice. 'I demand that everyone leaves those gloomy walls within which these tyrannical laws prevail. Let them embrace a simple and peaceful life under the vault of heaven.'

The members listened but made no reply. They were curious what John would say next. The church was his next target. John believed the main reason why the church was so corrupt was because it was far too rich. There was nothing in the Scriptures to excuse the church's bad behaviour, nor to justify why the church was so wealthy. Therefore John appealed to the king to take possession of the church's properties, as the church was under his authority.

Parliament liked that argument. Anything that placed the king in charge of his kingdom was usually well received. Tithes and offerings were John's next topic for change.

'An attack on the friars again,' he heard a member of the House mumble to his neighbour.

'Yes, good sir,' he retorted, looking at the member directly. 'The friars are dangerous. They do nothing but stuff the people with garbage.'

John believed that tithes and offerings should only be given to someone according to their needs. They should be given to help the priest get on with his work in an honest fashion. But if any priest was found to be unworthy of their position, then he should not receive any support.

'I demand that the poor inhabitants of our towns and villages should not be forced to support an ungodly priest,' he said sternly. 'Such a man is often vicious and a false teacher. Any tithes or offerings provide him with the means of satisfying his gaudiness, his greed, and his immorality, by buying a showy horse, expensive saddles, bridles with dangling bells, rich clothes, and soft furs, while they watch the wives and children of their neighbours dying with hunger!' he bellowed. John felt very strongly about this.

There were murmurings of agreement from parliament. John's appeal was not finished. He came at last to the primary issue that forced his appeal to king and parliament — his challenge to the 'real presence' of Christ in the bread and wine of the Eucharist. John believed the church's teaching about this was particularly dangerous and of the devil.

'Satan tricks the faithful of the church with the help of his deputy, Antichrist, to persuade everyone that the bread is not truly bread, but just looks like bread,' John said. 'If he can do that, there is no limit to anything that he can persuade the people to believe, because there is nothing more opposed to Scripture or to the discernible person than the devilish doctrine of transubstantiation. So, let the life of a cardinal or bishop be whatever he wants it to be. He can be guilty of a luxurious lifestyle. He can be guilty of murder. But the people can be led to believe that he is not like that. They may even be persuaded to believe that the Pope is infallible[1] in matters of the Christian faith. And because

---

1. *Infallible* means 'without error'. Five hundred years later, the Roman Catholic Church declared that the Pope was *infallible* at the First Vatican Council (1869-1870).

he is called the 'Most Holy Father', he is of course, free from sin!' he said with exasperation in his voice. He really wanted people to use their minds when they studied the Bible. So, if the church could impose the belief of transubstantiation on the nation, John feared there was no limit to what the church could persuade people to believe.

Dr Wycliffe's attack on the doctrine and practices of the Church of Rome was astounding. Those who supported his stand against papal taxations in the past were no longer by his side the moment he challenged the church's teaching of transubstantiation. It didn't matter to John that they stopped supporting him. It didn't matter that he was alone because the truth was that John never felt alone – the Lord Jesus was always with him. The Lord gave him the strength and courage to take a firm stand in the middle of all the relentless opposition.

When parliament heard the appeal, they did not deliberate long. Much to the annoyance of his enemies, John won his cause. The ruling pronounced by King Richard at Blackfriars was overturned.

All eyes now turned to the Archbishop of Canterbury, William Courtenay. What would he do with John? What could he do?

The only course of action was to look to the convocation, the church's parliament, for support in his attempt to discipline John for his rebellious stance against the church's hierarchy and doctrines.

Courtenay called the meeting in Oxford, the place where John shone most brightly in the past. Chancellor Rygge was aware that all personal support for John had slipped away. As a matter of self-preservation, Rygge decided it was prudent to be an obedient servant of the archbishop and the Convocation, along with the overabundance of bishops, Doctors of Divinity and other clergy who would act as John's judges.

Once again, John stood before Courtenay. The focus of this trial was transubstantiation, again. All his enemies wanted to know was if John affirmed or denied the church's teaching on this fundamental doctrine? John was not intimidated by his surroundings. He remained consistent in his position which had been shown plainly to him from the Scriptures.

'There is no "fleshly" presence of Christ in the sacrament, only a spiritual one,' he said, reaffirming his position on the issue. There was an angry murmur from his judges, but John continued to speak in a loud voice, 'And those who affirm the Church of Rome's position on this are themselves, false teachers.'

The volume of dissenting voices increased. Courtenay called for calm and got it straightaway. He looked menacingly at John, but before he could say anything in response to John's remarks, John spoke again, only this time his tone was soft.

'With whom do you think you are contending?' he asked, as he looked at the faces of his judges. 'Do you think you are contending with an old man who is physically weak and on the brink of the grave? No,' he said shaking his head, 'You are contending with truth.' John raised a finger and began pointing at his accusers. 'Truth,' he repeated, 'which is stronger than you and will overcome you.'

The room was silent. Not a word was spoken, not even a vicious jibe from Courtenay. With these words, John walked out of the council and went back to Lutterworth. He would never return to Oxford.

Archbishop Courtenay got the outcome he desired from his hand-picked judges. If Lollardy ever raised its head again in Oxford it would be crushed. It was clear that there was no freedom to discuss doctrine openly in the university anymore.

***

At Lutterworth, John continued his work of training preachers while the good Lord gave him the strength to do it. His 'Bible Men' continued to preach throughout the land. Although he was getting weaker, he was able to write some more books, including one that argued against the doctrine of transubstantiation. It was called "The Wicket". But on the last Sunday of 1384, during a service of the Lord's Supper, John collapsed in front of his congregation. It was his third stroke.

Parishioners scrambled to help him. He was lifted gently into a chair and taken slowly and carefully out of the church building through a side door and in to the rectory close by. John Purvey and some other men helped their dying rector into bed. Purvey remained at his bedside while the others left quietly.

Purvey looked at his frail friend and mentor lying motionless in his bed. The stroke left John mute. He had uttered his last words during the Lord's Supper. Over the next two days, Purvey did everything he could to make John's last moments as comfortable as possible.

It was on the last day of December 1384, that John Wycliffe died peacefully in bed at the rectory of Lutterworth. Soon after his body was laid to rest in the adjoining graveyard at Lutterworth.

***

The Council of Constance met on 14th May 1415. The council's purpose was to convict men of heresy. The council examined the writings of Dr Wycliffe and concluded that there were 260 counts of false teaching within them. Dr Wycliffe was condemned as the main leader of heresy during his lifetime. The usual punishment for heretics was to burn them, so the Council of Constance ordered that John's bones be dug up and burned. The council also ordered that Dr Wycliffe's books were to be burned, for fear that his writings could lead faithful Roman Catholic people astray.

At that time, Lutterworth lay in the Diocese of Lincoln. The Bishop of Lincoln was Philip Repton who was sympathetic to Dr Wycliffe's teaching. As a younger man, Repton was one of Wycliffe's 'Bible Men' but had later renounced this position. Still, Repton ignored the order from the Council of Constance concerning Dr Wycliffe's exhumation and burning. So nothing was done until Repton's successor came into the Diocese of Lincoln. He was called Richard Fleming. On 9th December 1427, Bishop Fleming gave the order for Dr Wycliffe's bones to be dug up and publicly burned in Lutterworth. The executioners were told to get rid of Dr Wycliffe's ashes once and for all. So they poured his ashes into the town's River Swift.

***

It was not enough for John Wycliffe to write the truth. He believed that the truth must also be lived. He was thoroughly consistent in his behaviour which made it very difficult for his enemies to find fault with his life.

John persevered in his work to preach the Word of God clearly and he eagerly sought to train others up to do the same. He was a true servant of the living God and trusted wholeheartedly in the promises of God throughout his life. He was a true pastor with a heart for the poorer in society.

John loved the Bible and lived his life in obedience to it. He was bold in his stance for Christ, and he had the courage to resist the false claims of the Church of Rome. He was constantly oppressed by the hierarchy of the church. In the end he was deserted by his followers and left to fight for truth on his own.

He wondered if he might die a martyr's death, but he was ready for that outcome if it came. 'To live and be silent, is impossible for me,' he said. 'The guilt of such treason against the Lord of heaven is more to be dreaded than many deaths.'

Although John did not die a martyr's death, his enemies showed how much they hated him by what they did to his bones. They may have got rid of his ashes, but they were unable to stop John's influence, even beyond the grave.

John Wycliffe has been hailed the 'Grandfather of the Reformation' because his Biblical teachings were embraced and used by the Bohemian reformer John Huss, and then by Martin Luther in Germany[2]. A manuscript in Prague illustrates the point; of John Wycliffe striking a spark, John Huss kindling the coals, and Martin Luther brandishing a flaming torch.

The picture speaks of the wonderful and amazing works of God in bringing his gospel to the world through brave, faithful, and godly servants of the Lord. John Wycliffe was such a servant of God. He was a man who was 'filled with the knowledge of his will in all spiritual wisdom and understanding, so as to walk in a manner worthy of the Lord, fully pleasing to him, bearing fruit in every good work and increasing in the knowledge of God' (Colossians 1:9-10).

2. For more information, see *Martin Luther - Reformation Fire* by Catherine Mackenzie in the Trail Blazer series of Christian Focus Publications.

Fact File
The Black Death

The Black Death is said to have been the worst disaster in history. It killed about 25 million people in Europe and countless millions in Asia. It was a form of bubonic plague. It got its name from the spots of blood that formed under the skin and turned black. The first symptoms were swelling of the groin and armpits. Victims usually died within a few hours.

The plague was carried by rat fleas which could also live on humans. Bubonic plague is not carried by human contact, but later the Black Death turned into a pneumonic plague. That meant it could be transferred through the air, and it spread from person to person.

Some historians believe that the disease was carried by a Mongolian raiding party from central Asia to the Crimea. From there it spread to the Mediterranean by ships. The Black Death arrived in Genoa in Italy in 1347. Then it travelled west and north, to Paris and London in 1348, and to Scandinavia and northern Russia in 1349. It devastated vast areas. Many homes, towns and villages were abandoned. Corpses of victims lay unburied in open fields.

The effects of the Black Death were widespread. Before the plague, there were many labourers who worked for low wages. After the plague, the shortage of workers was everywhere. As a result, wages rose rapidly. There were attempts to keep wages low, but this often led to revolts, for example the Peasants Revolt of 1381 in England.

The Avignon Papacy

In 1302 Pope Boniface VIII issued a bull called the 'Unam Sanctum' which means 'One Holy'. In this bull, the Pope stated that all worldly powers were subject to the one holy, spiritual authority, as empowered in the Pope. 'We declare that it is altogether necessary to salvation for every human creature to be subject to the Roman pontiff,' declared the Pope in the 'Unam Sanctum' bull.

The arrogance of the Pope's claims angered many rulers but none more so than Philip the Fair, King of France. He summoned the first meeting of the 'States-General of France', in which clergy, nobles and ordinary French folk appeared. This assembly supported the king and opposed the Pope. Boniface was captured and died soon afterwards, possibly from shock, because he was a very old man.

Soon after this, in 1309, Pope Clement V moved his papal court from Rome to Avignon in France. This was the beginning of what Roman Catholic historians have called the 'Babylonian Captivity' of the church. It lasted for nearly seventy years.

During that time, the Popes were mostly nominated by the French king and were in essence the king's servants. England was also involved in the 'Hundred Years' War' with France. Therefore any French Pope was unlikely to have sympathy with an English reformer like John Wycliffe.

Statutes of Provisors and Praemunire

The Statute of Provisors was a law that was passed by parliament in 1351. This law was intended to stop the Pope appointing foreign clergy to English benefices, that is, well-paid positions in the church in England.

The Statutes of Praemunire were laws that were passed in 1353 and 1365 by parliament. These laws were intended to stop papal bulls and directives from the Pope being carried out in England unless parliament endorsed them.

These laws were not strictly enforced in England and did little to stop the corruption they were designed for. That was because King Edward III wanted to keep some sort of working relationship with the papacy during his reign.

A third Statute of Praemunire was passed by parliament in 1393. This law gave heavy penalties for anyone who bought or gave out papal bulls; or pronounced sentences of excommunication from the church; or who engaged in any act that paid no attention to the authority and rights of the English monarchy.

Hundred Years' War

The Hundred Years' War between England and France was not one long war. That would be exhausting. Rather, it was a series of short wars. It started in 1337 and ended in 1453. That means the conflict actually lasted one hundred and sixteen years. English kings tried to dominate France, while the French tried to throw the English out of England!

In 1328 Charles IV of France died without an heir to his throne. French nobility enthroned his cousin, Philip VI. However, the nephew of Charles IV challenged Philip's right to be king. Charles's nephew was called Edward III of England. When Philip confiscated Edward's lands in France, war broke out.

The English defeated a French fleet in the English Channel at *Sluys* near France. The English then went on to invade and they won a large land battle at *Crecy* in 1346. At this battle, an English army of ten thousand men defeated a French army twice the size. The English longbow archers were much better than the French archers who used crossbows. Edward III then went on to capture *Calais* in northern France. However, both armies ran out of money. So they called a truce that lasted from 1347 until 1355.

In 1355 a fresh English invasion took place. This time it was led by Edward III's son who was also called Edward. He had the nickname of 'The Black Prince' because of the colour of his armour – it was black. Prince Edward won a great victory at *Poitiers* in the west-central part of France. He captured Philip VI's heir, who was John II of France, and put him in prison back in London, England.

The 'Treaty of Bretigny' in 1360 gave England large parts of France. However, a new war campaign followed this peace treaty and England lost most of the land it held in France.

For a while, the French and English thrones were occupied by children. In England, the ten-year-old Richard II was crowned king in 1377. His uncle, John of Gaunt, basically ruled in his place for the first few years of his reign. Gaunt was thought to be the most powerful man in England at the time. Charles VI of France was only eleven years old when he came to the throne in 1380.

A truce was agreed between the two nations when Richard II married Isabella, the daughter of Charles VI in 1396. King Richard was twenty two years older than Isabella when they were married. She was only six years old!

John of Gaunt, the Duke of Lancaster

England and France were at war again in 1369. England had very little money to pay for the war. The government tried to raise funds by taxing the English people. Many clergy held high positions in government, but they were exempt from paying more taxes. The English people were very angry about the situation, because as far as they were concerned, these clergy were raising taxes which they didn't have to pay! As a result, the people of England began to develop bad feelings towards the clergy in England, and their leader the Pope.

The following year, 1370, this bad 'anti-clerical' feeling swept through the nation. By now, John of Gaunt was a very influential and powerful man in England. He used the 'anti-clerical' feeling of the people to gain more influence and power. He managed to have certain clerics removed from their high positions in the government and he replaced them with his own loyal men.

So in 1371, William Wykeham, the Bishop of Winchester, resigned his high position in government as Lord Chancellor. Thomas de Brantingham, the Bishop of Exeter, resigned his high position in government as Treasurer as well. All other bishops and clergy who held any position in the government resigned too.

Gaunt then influenced the nobility, who were responsible for making the new appointments, to place his loyal men in those positions vacated by the outgoing clergy. Gaunt's goal was to intensify the long-standing argument between the Church of Rome and the English Parliament. The bishops held Gaunt responsible for the change and distrusted him intensely.

Then in the autumn of 1376, there was a meeting of a great council which gathered to convict William Wykeham, the Bishop of Winchester, on charges of corruption during his time as Lord Chancellor. The council found him guilty of corruption. However, Wykeham used his privileges as Bishop of Winchester to avoid spending any time in prison. Instead he was banished from the king's court, and all his worldly goods were taken off him. The bishops blamed Gaunt for their colleague's downfall and disliked him for it.

Later on, Gaunt was believed to be the chief supporter of a proposed law that was put before parliament. If the law was passed, it would have transferred all power from the Mayor of London into the hands of his loyal friend, Lord Percy, the King's Marshal. The people of London heard about this proposed law. They disliked Gaunt for his unquenchable thirst for power, and for seeking to meddle with their lives and freedoms.

John of Gaunt eventually became the most powerful man in England, thanks to the young age of King Richard II when he was crowned. As the king's uncle, Gaunt became the king's regent from 1377–1386.

The Normans

On 14th October 1066, there was a fierce battle at Hastings on the south coast of England. It was fought between the armies of William, the Duke of Normandy in France, and Harold II who was the King of England.

King Harold was killed, and the English army was defeated. On Christmas Day in 1066, William of Normandy was crowned King William I of England at Westminster Abbey in London, England. The people who followed King William from Normandy in France to live in England were called 'The Normans'.

At first many people in the north and east of England rebelled against King William's rule. However, King William quashed the rebellions in those parts of England. He took the land and gave it to his followers. He gave a lot of land to the Church and replaced most of the English bishops with French ones. King William also encouraged traders and craftsmen from France to settle and work in England.

During William's reign as king, everyday life in England and Wales began to change. The Normans built large castles. Towns grew up around them. Old churches were replaced with bigger ones. Great cathedrals were built. Monasteries and convents were set up by monks and nuns from France. New followers were attracted to these religious orders from the local areas.

French became the major language of the gentry in England. It was spoken at the royal court. It was spoken by the gentry and the clergy. It was also used in the courts of law. Literature was translated into French, including the Bible. Only the nation's wealthy could afford a Bible in French. Many people chose to learn French to get greater wealth and higher social status. But the majority of the population continued to speak English.

Although life under the Normans was harsh at times, it did bring some advantages. A castle could provide protection for the locals against anyone who attacked them. In 1085 King William ordered a survey of all the land in England. He wanted to find out who lived where, how much the land was worth, and how much tax he could get from the people who lived there.

Transubstantiation

The main reason why reformers like John Wycliffe were accused and burned for heresy (that is, teaching against the false doctrines of the Church of Rome) was because they refused to believe in one unusual doctrine of the Roman Catholic Church. For the reformers like John Wycliffe, life or death hinged on this doctrine. If they believed it, they lived. If they didn't, they died.

The doctrine was the *real presence* of the body and blood of Jesus Christ in the consecrated bread and wine in the Lord's Supper (also known as the Mass, or Holy Communion, or the Eucharist – which means 'thanksgiving').

In Anglo-Saxon times, the doctrine of transubstantiation was not accepted in the church. Aelfric the Abbot of St Albans taught that the bread 'is the body of Christ, not bodily, but spiritually.'

After the Norman conquest, new bishops arrived in England. A man called Lanfranc became the Archbishop of Canterbury. He claimed that when the priest said the words of consecration during the Mass, Christ left heaven and descended to the altar. Eventually this doctrine of transubstantiation was widely accepted by the Church of Rome.

John Wycliffe denied this doctrine. He argued that the doctrine of transubstantiation was not supported in the Bible or in the traditions of the early church. He said, 'The consecrated host (that is, the bread and wine that has been set apart as holy) we see upon the altar (table) is neither Christ, nor any part of him, but an effectual sign of him.'

Wycliffe's view was the same as Martin Luther's, the continental reformer of the sixteenth century. It was called 'consubstantiation' – that Christ's body and blood are present 'with, in and under' the bread and wine, instead of replacing them altogether. Later Reformers, like John Calvin and Ulrich Zwingli, rejected this position.

The Hierarchy of the Roman Catholic Church (ranked highest to lowest)

Pope – the head of the Roman Catholic Church.

Cardinal - a senior member of the clergy and advisor to the Pope.

Archbishop – the highest ranking bishop of a large district or area called a 'diocese'.

Bishop – has authority over the priests and parishes in his diocese.

Priest – a member of the clergy who has been ordained by the Roman Church to perform certain religious ceremonies, such as the Mass.

Wycliffe Church Inscription: Lutterworth Parish Church, 1837.

Sacred to the memory of John Wiclif,

The earliest champion of ecclesiastical reformation in England. He was born in Yorkshire in the year 1324, In the year 1375 he was presented to the rectory of Lutterworth: Where he died on the 31st December 1384,

At Oxford he acquired not only the renown of a consummate schoolman, But the far more glorious title of the Evangelical Doctor

His whole life was one impetuous struggle against the corruptions And encroachments of the Papal Court, And the impostures of its devoted auxiliaries, the mendicant fraternities.

His labours in the cause of scriptural truth Were crowned by one immortal achievement, His translation of the Bible into the English tongue. His mighty work drew him on, indeed, the bitter hatred Of all who were making merchandize of the popular credulity and ignorance: But he found an abundant reward in the blessing of his countrymen,

Of every rank and age, to whom he unfolded the words of eternal life. His mortal remains were interred near this spot: But they were not allowed to rest in peace: After the lapse of many years, His bones were dragged from the grave, and consigned to the flames: And his ashes were cast into the waters of the adjoining stream.

(From John Wycliffe, *The Dawn of the Reformation*, by David Fountain, page 71)

John Wycliffe
Timeline

1324   John Wycliffe born in the village of 'Wycliffe' in Yorkshire.

1340   Entered the University of Oxford.

1348   The Black Death arrived in England.

1351   First Statute of Provisors was passed by parliament.

1353   First Statute of Praemunire was passed by parliament.

1356   Awarded B.A. degree.

1358   Awarded M.A. degree.

1360   Published 'Objection to the Friars'.

1361   Appointed as Rector of Fillingham in Lincolnshire, England.

1365   Second Statute of Praemunire passed by parliament.

1372   Awarded Doctor of Divinity degree. Wycliffe also became a Professor of Divinity.

1374   Appointed as Rector of Lutterworth (Church inscription at Lutterworth dates it as 1375). Wycliffe was a King's Commissioner which met the papal delegation in Bruges.

1376   The Good Parliament.

1377   Pope Gregory XI issued 'papal bulls' against John Wycliffe.

1377   King Edward III died on 1st June. Richard II now King of England, aged ten.

1378   The Papal Schism. Pope Gregory XI died.

1381   The Peasants' Revolt.

1382   The Blackfriars' Synod.

1382   Latin Vulgate Bible translated into English.

1384   John Wycliffe died on 31st December in his home in Lutterworth, England.

1410   Books written by John Wycliffe were burned in Oxford.

1414   Council of Constance. Wycliffe declared a 'heretic'.

1427   Wycliffe's bones were dug up and burned. His ashes were scattered into the River Swift.

Thinking Further Topics

Chapter One – The Great Plague
When John saw people die because of the plague, he turned to God for comfort and strength. How do you react to bad situations around you? Do you turn to God in times of trouble? Read Psalm 130.

Chapter Two – The Poor Friars
John warned against false teaching in the church. Do you think false teaching still happens in churches today? How can you recognise it? Read Acts 17:10-15 and 1 Timothy 1:3-11 to start you thinking about this.

Chapter Three – The Oxford Scholar
Throughout John's adult life, England was at war with France. Today there are wars and rumours of wars around the world. Do you think God is still in control of his world, or not? Read Psalm 46.

Chapter Four – The Evangelical Doctor
John wrote a book about the Ten Commandments. Do you think the Ten Commandments are still important today? Read Exodus 20:1-17 and Matthew 22:34-40.

Chapter Five – The King's Commissioner
John believed that God knew what was best for him in his life. Do you believe that God knows what is best for

his children? Read Luke 11:1-13 to get you thinking about this.

Chapter Six – The Papal Adversary

John did not believe that Christ's church should be wealthy. He wanted to see money used for the purpose of gospel ministry and for the poor of society. Do you agree? Read Luke 16:1-13 carefully to help you think clearly about how to use your money.

Chapter Seven – The Lambeth Trial

John would not be deterred from teaching the Bible by the churchmen opposed to him. Have you ever been tempted to keep quiet about the gospel for fear of what your friends might think, say, or do to you? Read Acts 5:17-42.

Chapter Eight – The Bedside Visit

The men who visited John when he was ill were full of hypocrisy. What do you think hypocrisy is? What does Jesus say about how to avoid hypocrisy? Read Matthew 6:1-18 to get you thinking.

Chapter Nine – The English Bible

John believed that the Bible should be the ultimate authority for God's church, and that God's people should do what the Word of God says. Is the Bible important to you? If so, why? Read Deuteronomy 8:3

and Matthew 4:1-11. What is the attitude of Jesus to the Scriptures?

Chapter Ten – The Bible Men
John wanted his 'Bible Men' to be good role models in their Christian ministry. Do you have a good Christian role model in your life? If so, can you think what makes him or her a good role model? Read Philippians 2:19-30. How are Timothy and Epaphroditus good role models for the Philippian church?

Chapter Eleven – The Earthquake Synod
Why was it so important to John that the people of England had a translation of the Bible in their own language? Do you pray for the people who translate the Bible into different languages from around the world? Read Psalm 119 – take your time, it's a long one.

Chapter Twelve – The Heavenly Call
John was only sixty years old when he died. He was not afraid to die because he knew he was going to heaven. Do you know where you are going when you die? Read Philippians 3:12-20 and John 11:25-26. What does Jesus say about death here?

OTHER BOOKS IN THE
TRAIL BLAZERS SERIES

For a full list of Trail Blazers, please see our website:
www.christianfocus.com
All Trail Blazers are available as e-books

Other books by the author ...

Thomas Cranmer moved amongst Kings and Queens, influencing the throne of England and the centre of national power. But he lived at a time when the power of the monarch was absolute and the decisions you made were a matter of life and death. Cranmer's life is perhaps best known for a decision he made that he later regretted and deeply repented of. But his final legacy is the truth that he held on to the last.

ISBN: 978-1-5271-0877-6

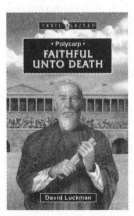

Polycarp was Bishop of Smyrna (a city in modern–day Turkey) in the days of the early church. He was a disciple of the apostle John. He was martyred in his eighties for refusing to burn incense to the Roman emperor. David Luckman's new biography in the Trail Blazer series shows readers how this brave man's faith was the most important thing to him.

ISBN: 978-1-5271-1029-8

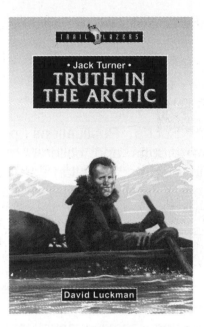

TRAIL BLAZERS

• Jack Turner •
TRUTH IN
THE ARCTIC

David Luckman

Jack Turner was a trained pharmacist and pastor who went to the Arctic to translate God's Word into the native language. It was a world of snow and hunting and anyone who lived there had to become familiar with the ways of living in the Arctic. Ten weeks out of every year the sun never set and for three months the world was in complete darkness.

The spiritual darkness of the North was being pushed back by the power of the gospel and the Lord Jesus Christ that Jack Turner followed. But danger is around every corner in the wild North – and Jack runs into trouble.

ISBN: 978-1-5271-0792-2

CHRISTIAN FOCUS PUBLICATIONS

Christian Focus | Christian Heritage | CF4K | Mentor

Christian Focus Publications publishes books for adults and children under its four main imprints: Christian Focus, CF4K, Mentor and Christian Heritage. Our books reflect our conviction that God's Word is reliable and Jesus is the way to know him, and live for ever with him.

Our children's publication list covers pre-school to early teens. We also publish personal and family devotional titles, biographies and inspirational stories that children will love.

From pre-school board books to teenage apologetics, we have it covered!

Find us at our web page:
www.christianfocus.com

CF4•K
Because you're never
too young to know Jesus